Opening Closed Doors

Case Histories of a Palmist-Clairvoyant

Leonard Flint Ritson

Leonard Flint Ritson
1986

EBA

Eric Bruton Associates Ltd,
Ipswich, Suffolk

First Published in 1985

PUBLISHER'S NOTE

While all the incidents described in this book are based on actual case histories, all the forenames and surnames of the people described in them and, in nearly every instance, the careers or professions of the individuals mentioned, have been changed to protect their identity. The Publishers wish to emphasise therefore that the references have no connection whatever with any person who, by coincidence, may bear an identical or similar name.

British Library Cataloguing in Publication Data

Ritson, Leonard Flint
Opening closed doors : case histories of a palmist-clairvoyant.
1. Clairvoyance
I. Title
133.8'4'0924 BF1281

ISBN 0-7198-0034-X

Text input by Eric Bruton Associates Ltd. Typeset by Budget Typesetting Ltd, Beckenham, Kent. Printed and bound in Great Britain by Anchor Brendon Ltd, Tiptree, Colchester, Essex.

Contents

List of Illustrations

I dedicate this book to Cis, and to my clients, for without them it would not have been possible to express all that has been written within these covers.

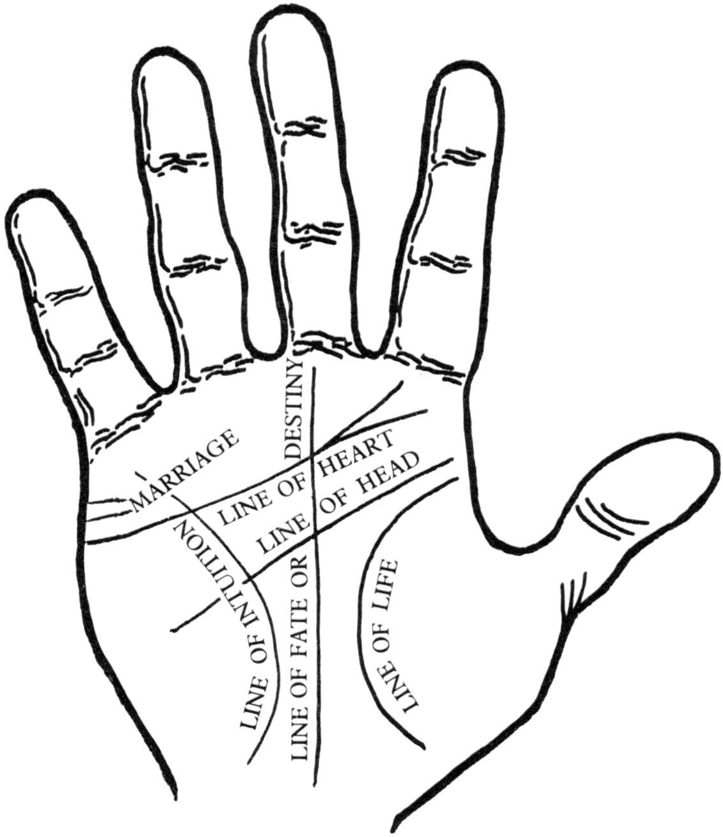

THE PRINCIPAL LINES OF THE HAND

Line of Head: indicates principally the mentality of the subject, degree of intelligence, temperament and talent.

Line of the Heart: known also as the mensal, relates to emotional and sexual expression of the subject, the degree of passion, pride and jealousy existing in their nature.

Line of Life: refers to a person's vitality, resistance to disease or illness. This line does not indicate longevity.

▷ *Page 8*

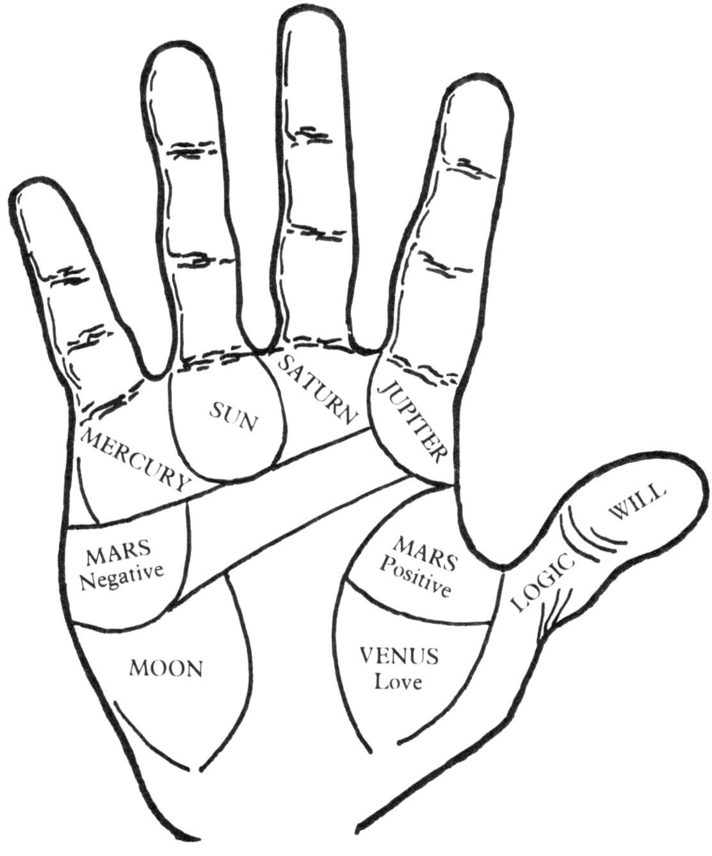

THE MOUNTS OF THE HAND

The names were first given to the mounts by the Greeks, who associated them with the qualities of the seven planets, and which are:

Mercury: wit, alertness of thought especially to commerce and science, love of travel, change and excitation.

Sun: artistic calling, mental grace, attraction to literature and poetry.

Saturn: solitude, earnestness, prudence, an interest in that which is sombre.

▷ *Page 8*

The Principal Lines of the Hand

Line of Fate or Destiny: pertains to all worldly affairs, how influences, good or bad, contribute to the life-style of the subject and their acceptance or otherwise to that which befalls them.

Line of Intuition: refers to a person's impressionable nature, how much they exhibit an intuitional instinct of presentiment which, if developed, could enable them to be psychic.

Line of Marriage: alludes to romantic liaisons, affairs of the heart, marriage ceremonies and the influence of certain people during the subject's life.

The Mounts of the Hand

Jupiter: desire for power, ambition, vigour and enthusiasm.

Mars Positive: courageous, persistent if not argumentative.

Mars Negative: resignation, self-control, keen sense of justice.

Moon, known also as Luna: denotes imagination, refinement, keen appreciation of beauty in art, literature and nature.

Venus: passion, sensuality, love of music, colour and beauty. The larger the mount, the stronger the passion and tendency towards sexual domination.

Logic: having a waist-like appearance indicates tact, whereas more full and clumsy shows force in achieving any set purpose.

Will: if flat it shows calm, controlled reasoning; when thick or heavy, this denotes ungovernable passion or will-power.

Preface

WHAT is described in the following pages is not a textbook of palmistry. The case histories presented show how varied is the nature of some people's problems, their choices and reactions and, more important, how useful palmistry can be for everyone. It offers us the chance to know ourselves better, and to appreciate the scope and role open to us in life; and it helps us to a better understanding of those close to us, as well as providing a sense of personal accomplishment in the midst of whatever life holds in store.

Hand interpretation is both a science and an art, and the technique is known by the name of chirology. A chirologist, or palmist, uses two analytical systems in this particular study of human nature, in which the hand is a map. The insight into a person's true personality, potential, past, present, and future life is obtained by cheirognomy, the study of the shape of the hands, fingers and skin texture: and by cheiromancy, the study of the lines and markings upon the palmar surface of the hand. These two systems complement each other to provide information for an assessment of the individual's strengths and weaknesses.

I practise what is known as divinatory palmistry, which is a combination of palmistry and clairvoyance. The case histories described in this book are examples of the types of situations I have dealt with in the course of fifteen years' work experience.

The method I operate is one where I examine both of my client's hands at the same time. I begin with close inspection of the left hand using a large magnifying glass, followed by a closer inspection of the right hand. I make a note of any visible contrasts, changes or modifications that occur in relation to each palm, after which I use the right hand as the basis of my reading. Then at any point where appropriate during the hand analysis I may introduce clairvoyance to help give a more detailed and accurate picture.

The lines and markings on the left hand show whether a person possesses power or influence, and reveal information about his or her early life. We learn the basic destiny of that individual: that is, how they could have lived their life had they awaited events and not resisted any opportunities offered.

The right hand reflects changes caused by ambition or lack of it, and through the influences of people around them. For that matter, one dominant person in particular could have been influential in causing alterations to the person's original choice of life-style or attitude.

Change can also occur for the individual through opportunities, happenings or events which develop out of the blue and have no real connection with any previous experience in a person's life. The relationship between what the left hand signifies and what the right hand contains within its signs is a living effect, manifest in both hands throughout a person's lifetime, reflecting the contrasts of both cause and effect.

Should both left and right hands bear the same marking or sign upon them in a precisely corresponding position, then the significance of those markings is accepted by the chirologist as a confirmed state, whether in the person's past or present way of life, or in that which is to come.

Palmistry can be approached in various correlations, in terms of the hands and the physical or mental states, for the practice of medical and therapeutic cheiromancy. Another correlation involves hands and character assessment, which is psycho-therapeutic cheiromancy. Yet another correlation is that of the hands and the past, present or future, which is divinatory cheiromancy. Although palmistry is a rational science, there are those who, like myself, believe that clairvoyance can be of value in the process of interpretation.

Because opinions and conclusions regarding technique depend so much on the individual, chirologists must select for themselves the method designed to give the best results from the hand-reading. They should also have the wisdom to avoid being drawn into a superficial assessment which flatters the subject, and is based mainly on stressing virtues.

The rich and varied nature of the problems which people encounter builds into a unique panorama which confronts and challenges an analyst such as myself. A striking feature which I have observed in the course of my work is the frequency with which one person's life is so like that of another, in the sense that they run similar, near parallel courses, yet each is totally unknown to the other.

Individuals functioning independently in their own way and living their own lives, nevertheless encounter problems of an identical nature, as is to be expected. In many cases, their response or reactions to these problems follow a similar pattern. As to how the problem is solved, each person has his or her own particular stamp which leaves its mark and, inexorably, it is fate or destiny which has the final word.

The following case histories are based on real life stories, but all the names and details of occupations and life styles have been changed to protect the identity of the people involved.

Today

The language of the hand, it speaks
To those who know the signs
In the pattern of the lines
Upon an outstretched palm
Of one most eager then to know
Which way they go.

So each man's life,
With that too of his wife
And child newborn,
Is stamped upon their skin;
All terms of fate
That few can read.

'Stranger, before it is too late
Tell me what you see,
And so give up to me
Life's ancient key,
My destiny.'

CHAPTER 1
Allowing for the Unexpected

CLIENTS come to me from all walks of life and for a variety of reasons. There are those who believe that extra-sensory perception works and is of value; there are those people who want to believe and are not sure. Also there are those who do not believe in any such thing, but nevertheless find themselves sitting opposite me for a consultation which can reveal certain things about themselves of which they were not aware.

The sitter is as important as the medium. A receptive person is a good subject, and rapport can be established between the seeker and the seer. The gullible client however, hanging on every word or phrase the medium utters, can make mistakes by misinterpretation; or, through their own confusion, miss chances of progress and enlightenment, for which the medium is not to blame. Sceptics often are an interesting challenge, I find, and if they can be once shown the effectiveness of extra-sensory perception, they usually remain converted.

Imagine being told the following. 'You are too fond of speed: you drive too fast. I see you driving alone down a country road. It has been raining and the road surface is wet and slippery. You are quite familiar with the road along which you are travelling, as you have used the route a number of times before. Ahead is a very sharp double bend which you are approaching with deceptive swiftness. Your car is still travelling too fast. You negotiate one bend, start braking but cannot control the car around the second bend. The car begins to skid. Now you are out of control. It is your own fault. You are completely on your own; no other vehicle is involved. You are seconds away from injury, possibly death. The direction of the skid, taking you relentlessly towards a large tree which has a wide bole. There is no way you can avoid the impact. Here it comes. Now!'

A sceptic would not necessarily accept this information at first, if at all, let alone acknowledge it as an example of futuristic observation, offered on their behalf and clearly involving themselves.

Barry King was sceptical when, as part of a reading, I described to him a futuristic road accident, my intention being to prevent the incident by forewarning him, rather than confirming that it was likely to become a true happening in his life.

That which is destined to happen in a person's life will happen. Yet destiny will not necessarily appear to be working all the time through the events which confront an individual. We can determine for ourselves the direction we want to go in life by applying our free-will. Consequently if our free-will points us in one direction, yet that which is inevitable draws us in a totally different direction, then that which is fated or predestined will occur.

Should a person float upon a tide of circumstances which determine their purpose and style without any free-will of their own being evident, the emergence of ideas and situations not of their own making can often turn out to be for the better. Hence, an indecisive person could throw himself on destiny, and destiny would offer a better solution compared with other choices available to him. The blending of an individual's free-will (through which he can explore his potential and evolvement) with that which is inevitable and will not be denied, shapes the most natural pattern for a person's life-style.

The path of destiny

Destiny is inevitable and, hopefully, leads to achievement and wisdom, so that the role of errors, unhappiness and blockages to life development is seen more clearly after the event, but seldom before it. This is the functional interplay of the subjective part of nature related in turn to the objective pattern of the motive force of life.

Barry King did not believe that my description of a road accident could apply to him, because he did not want to accept that such a thing was possible. He tried to dismiss my observations with a display of humour which matched his extrovert nature. Yet barely one month after our consultation he paid me an unscheduled visit to tell me that, two weeks previously, part of what I had described had occurred. It was an experience that he was unlikely to forget.

'I cannot believe that it happened to me,' he said. 'I was driving alone down a country road in the afternoon. There had been some rain earlier, and the surface of the road was quite wet. I knew the road which I was travelling along well: I use it frequently in the course of my work. I drove up to this double bend. At the second bend the car began a long skid, and the brakes locked.

'As this was happening, everything around me seemed to occur in slow motion. Then I thought to myself, 'Blimey, that's what that palmist was telling me about.' My car skidded towards a tree at the side of the road. I managed to steer the car and narrowly missed hitting the tree. The car went through the hedgerow ending up at a standstill in a ploughed field. I was shaken, but otherwise unhurt. I just had to come and tell you how right you were.'

For myself, I was only too pleased that my prediction had not been correct in every detail. When something like this happens and I am describing a disturbing future event which registers for me as being more than a possibility, through an advance warning compatible with the details of the prediction, I am offering something to the client which is not part of his acknowledged consciousness. In doing so I am not sowing a seed of anxiety in the mind about the happening in advance in order to bring the event about.

In precognition, the medium is focusing on future out of the present. My technique is to use clairvoyance in conjunction with palmistry. In my reading of the palm, and being clairvoyant, I perceive symptoms parallel to those seen by a seer reading the crystal. The human mind functions in two ways: through its objective senses and through its subjective senses. Clairvoyance focuses on the subjective nature of the mind and translates it into objective terms.

The ability to see a picture with the mind's 'third eye', then to detect a sense, likening the picture to having a sound-track, and to draw on to a focal point of future, owes itself completely to subjective consciousness and to the spiritual laws which exist in the Universe. Clairvoyance is no less than a spiritual function to tune into the recording plane, being one of the solar planes of the universes of God.

If the acorn can have a brain which enables it when planted underground to locate the direction of the Sun, the power of the mind of man can focus on the finite and the infinite. What we commonly call a sixth sense can be incorporated within these functions. Cats develop and use a heightened awareness; so too can man. Given the facilities of greater awareness within his own power, man should use them.

The technique of divinatory palmistry, experienced as a combination of palmistry with clairvoyance, functions for me in the following way. When I first look in a client's hand, I see the lines upon the palmar surface as forming a map. It is important that I am relaxed and that my mind is clear of any set image at this point, and that I allow my concentration to build up so that it focuses instinctively or intuitively upon a particular area of the palm.

In this way, I can begin a straightforward hand-reading, apart from describing in a few sentences the client's character and personality, the nature of the immediate problem, if there is one, or the direction needed for certain achievements. For example, one client may have a business problem, or be faced with a professional or occupational proposition. Another client may be undergoing a period of marital difficulty, and I can predict whether or not the stresses involved would lead to the marriage ending in divorce.

In either of these cases, I can usually pin-point very early in the consultation the nature of the situation and any changes involved. I can also predict changes likely to confront them at certain periods in the future, without having to ask any questions whatsoever. In fact, I rarely ask my clients questions, because I accept the information I receive through my work. If I can give an unaided assessment, describing what the client is like as a person, and his capability in a particular context, then I can convince him as to the rightness or error of his ways.

Once a study of the lines in the hand has provided me with a basic map on which to build further observation, clairvoyance functions as an additional aid, extending the sensitivity of my mind, so that I am able to fill in the map. In this way a more concise and detailed picture of the happenings in my client's life can be formed, so that I can help to increase his understanding.

Clairvoyance can work on its own for me, though not necessarily to order. This sometimes happens unexpectedly, when I least anticipate being a receiver. At the moment of receiving the images which present themselves, I am almost oblivious of my surroundings. This is because I allow myself to be receptive to whatever images emerge, and I let the impulse lead the way.

Sound is known to be a vibration, proven by radio waves, which are the lowest frequencies of radiation within the electromagnetic spectrum. Increases of frequency produce infra-red radiation, light, x-rays, continuing up to the radiation associated with cosmic rays. Thought, indeed life itself, is a vibration, as is every human being. Clairvoyance can be termed vibratory in the sense that it is electromagnetic. And in applying my extra-sensory perception, part of my brain is attuned to absorb some of the particular pitch of which clairvoyance is composed.

When a certain strength of image is received, and provided the clairvoyant's mind is kept open and clear of personal thoughts, other images can follow the first in a rapidly-flowing sequence. The images which I perceive on these occasions are visual, present themselves in clear colours and are often accompanied by sound. Depending upon its nature, the sound can range from a whisper to a very distinct if not loud noise, which acts as a sound-track to accompany the picture shaped by clairvoyance.

The visual images are received in the centre of the forehead. The ancients referred to this zone as the 'third eye'. The visual imagery is termed clairvoyance, while audible imagery is known as clairaudience. I regard these as normal and acceptable functions within the scope of the human mind, which can be used or left alone. There should be nothing to fear from the use of these faculties, provided that they are used in a correct and sensible manner.

Direct images

With clairvoyance, the first clear image received should lead naturally thereon to a series of further images. Experience and testing will show whether a series of images is linked together directly, or whether a link can be identified after the event by appropriate analysis. Errors can arise if an attempt is made to make images fit together where they are not meant to be joined.

Direct, not imaginary, images are the ones that matter.

I can recall an instance where a client, while accepting the function of palmistry, did not believe in one of my predictions concerning her future. She was a person with charisma, who had a beautiful and expressive face. It was natural to her when speaking to use hand and arm gestures, in the manner of a Continental. She was an enthusiastic amateur opera singer, and though nature had given her rather a large figure, she was extremely light upon her feet.

The hand analysis and forecasts had been completed, and she came out of the consulting-room to join her friend, who had been waiting for her. She wore a flowing dress with a floral print design which suited her perfectly. Elegantly, she turned to me, and chuckled.

'You have been correct for the most part,' she said, 'but there is one thing about which you are quite wrong.' I let her continue. 'You tell me that I am going to have a baby; that is impossible. I am not pregnant, although I have been hoping to have a child for over ten years. Now my husband and I have given up trying.'

I approached her and made a rapid re- examination of her right hand in front of those present in the waiting-room. 'I see no reason to alter one word,' I told her. 'Your hand tells me that you are pregnant.' My pronouncement was greeted with self-conscious laughter by both women, and in a light-hearted mood they went their way.

I should point out that my readings are usually conducted in private, with only the client and myself present. If a client wishes to discuss what has been revealed to others afterwards, that is a matter outside my control.

The sequel was provided by the singer's friend, who came back for a consultation some months later. The singer had discussed the major points of my reading with her friend. I had advised her to go to have a medical examination, so that she would be well prepared for the birth of her baby, which I foresaw. She was reluctant to take my advice, but her friend convinced her that she should see her doctor, who confirmed that she was pregnant. Later, it was estimated that she could have been no more than five weeks pregnant at the time of her visit to me.

My client had her child and her world was complete. The years of frustration and waiting for her happy event had caused a form of mental blockage, a blind spot, so that she was incapable of believing that she could achieve motherhood. The sign upon her hand proved correct, and the third eye of clairvoyance was not blind to the meaning or the importance of this specific sign upon the palmar surface.

Cause and effect

The relationship between cause and effect is often more interesting. It was especially so in the life of Marjorie Powers, a level-headed young woman with a go-ahead personality, a happy marriage and two young children. She had been coming to me for consultations for a number of years, and her life for a time appeared to be orderly and well-run, even if she was occasionally restless and thought of resuming her career.

In my later readings, I found much information in her hands which involved her husband and his career prospects. Her attitude towards him was ambivalent. He was the key-stone in her life, and also dominated her. I do not think she was fully aware of this second fact. She seemed to feel that she was in charge of her life, and was going to make changes to suit herself, whereas what actually happened was very different.

I could see destiny intervening in her life between her subsconscious perception of her own potential, and her conscious reaction to practical changes demanded of her. I told her that I saw her husband, herself and their two children going to live in California because of her husband's promotion. At the same time, I advised her not to sell her house in England, but to use it for approximately one year as a second home, so that she would have a home to come back to if she changed her mind about living in America. I felt that her husband's financial position was sufficiently stable for them to be able to afford two homes, at least temporarily.

Marjorie was not prepared to accept my observations. 'My husband has reached as high as he can go in the firm which employs him. The company has no work or branches abroad, and there is no whisper of any such thing,' she retorted.

It seemed stange to her, but not to me, that she could return after a short time to confirm that the events I predicted were about to be set in motion. Her husband had been asked by his company to administer the export marketing of their food products which were about to be launched in the United States. The business was being based in California, and Marjorie's husband had gone there for six months, with an arrangement that his wife and children would follow later.

At a subsequent reading before she went abroad, I told her that she and her family would really enjoy their new life, and that after a year's trial they would come back to England only to sell their property and take leave of their relatives.

All this has taken place. Not too long ago I had a postcard from Marjorie showing a view of the Golden Bowl, and giving me the latest news. Outside events changed her life to a greater extent than she thought possible. There have been no regrets. Now, Marjorie is considering starting a business of her own.

Given that everyone born is an individual, the working of destiny is both singularly individual and collectively subtle in declaring its philosophy: a man can be an island if he wishes; yet the fulfilment of a person's aims may not come as a result of his solo efforts, but through links with others and through the contribution which they offer.

We have known cases where destiny was clearly marked upon the hand, and where every step was indicated from childhood onwards, and I have known others where only principal challenges or changes were detectable; and yet other clients whose situation remained undecided and stagnant for so long that their problems could only be resolved gradually, perhaps over a few years.

I recall a client in this category whom I have not seen for some time. Perhaps she does not need a consultation from me now, as her new life is secure and happy, and a far cry from its former style.

A certain lady decided in her late twenties to live with a man whom she thought she loved; and because he was unable to fend for himself she subsequently looked after him for over twenty years. They did not marry. The man was never in robust health so that any extra responsibilities and burdens became the woman's lot. Eventually he died, and his relatives claimed all of his belongings. The lady had to leave the home to which she had become attached, with very little money, or anything else to call her own.

I first met her when she was in this dilemma. In an analysis I was able to see a temporary home change for her, and this proved correct. From that point onwards the circumstances of her life improved. I told her that she would meet a man older than herself, a widower, that he would propose marriage, that she would accept his proposal, and her worries would be at an end.

The lady was shy, reserved, somewhat afraid to react favourably to the idea of courtship. But in a matter of months she met a man socially. They got on well together. Eventually they married and now seem to live only for each other. More happiness than she could anticipate has compensated this lady for her earlier suffering. Yet it was part and parcel of her destiny that such suffering should be a prelude to her ultimate peace and harmony.

The importance attached to prediction is determined by the extent to which a person accepts what is predicted. In some cases however the implications are not always recognised at once by the person for whom the prediction is made. I do not accept that prediction can be achieved by a medium through a process of mind reading. If the process were so simple, then any predictions could be upset if the subject chose to present a series of 'red herrings' to the medium.

Time will tell

If a prediction creates a mental image for the subject, which is quite unlike anything experienced previously, and subsequent events bear out the prophesy, the image cannot be said to have come about through the interplay of auto-suggestion. Yet in the post-prediction period, the subject's mind is likely to function along similar lines to the mode of thinking experienced initially by the medium. A mental parallel can be drawn between the time a prediction is uttered its achievement, and the state of mind of the subject experiencing the events predicted.

I first met Florence Chatterton on a day which I intended to spend leisurely. When she knocked at my door and politely asked for a reading, I weakened and invited her in. Though no longer young, she was a woman who took pride in her appearance and who could be flamboyant within her own circle of friends.

Her hands were inclined to be short, with well-formed, fleshy palms, and broadly- based fingers which tapered considerably towards the finger-tips. My first analysis revealed a symbolic build-up of change in her circumstances and life-style over a relatively short period, which I calculated as representing a two-and-half-year time zone immediately ahead of her. I described her then solitary nature. I said I thought she was a widow, and that I foresaw an imminent change of residence for her.

Florence Chatterton (she preferred to be called Flo) appeared to gain confidence as a result of my analysis, which she said was most helpful. From then onwards, events developed rapidly for her. At the time of my first reading, she was a widow preparing to retire from her job as a warden in a sheltered home for the elderly. Within two weeks she called again, this time to say that she had moved to a rented property in the locality.

Over the next year I saw Flo regularly on a social basis; she and Cis, my lady companion, became close friends. Within a year, without her mentioning it, I became aware that she was finding it increasingly difficult to manage financially. Accordingly her standard of living had begun to drop. I told Cis what I thought was happening, and arranged for my client to visit her at a time when they would be alone together. To ease Flo's financial situation, it was arranged that she became a home help to Cis for an agreed wage.

I was pleased at the pleasure they took in each other's company, but one day my intuition prompted me to give Cis a gentle warning against becoming too attached to Flo, as I felt that she would soon leave the country to live abroad. This impression was based on my recollection of what I first saw symbolised upon Flo's palm.

Though Cis found my comment hard to believe, information supporting my impression then came to light. One morning while helping Cis about the house, Flo announced that she was a New Zealander by birth. Up to that moment there had been nothing about her speech or behaviour to connect her with any place other than England. The inflection in her voice, her accent, was that of a Londoner. Her father had married a New Zealander but the marriage did not last. So as a little girl of eight she had sailed with her father to England.

When she had lived for two years in our locality, Flo took Cis and me into her confidence. She said she would sell the contents of her home and return to New Zealand. This was no surprise to me.

I read her hand before she left England. Palmistically by the form of her fate or destiny line upon her hand, she was answering a call deep-rooted in her subsconscious and clearly relating to her origin. She was past retirement age and was to most intents and purposes alone. I wanted her decision to remain her own, so I made no attempt to sway her one way or the other regarding its consequences. Privately, I thought her very brave to embark upon such an undertaking at her age, and I closely examined her hands for clues to the outcome of her proposed action.

I predicted that she would not be alone, but would have the aid of friends made upon her arrival in New Zealand. I foresaw a choice of at least two home moves, either of which could work out well for her. In addition there were clear indications of financial gains to improve her circumstances.

It transpired that her late husband had a nephew who had emigrated to New Zealand with his wife and family. By virtue of her mother's nationality, and because she qualified as a senior citizen, the New Zealand authorities gave Flo a pension, and made further concessions which enabled her to find a home. Finding that age was no barrier to employment for a fit person who wished to work, she took a job in a bank.

The last reading I gave her in England contained an unexpected surprise. I told her that I saw her marrying again, at which she giggled in disbelief. I challenged her doubt, explaining that I would not change what I saw. When I looked closer into the marriage theme with the aid of clairvoyance, I was given a name in Maori which sounded like 'Hawaii', but which I could neither spell nor pronounce correctly.

The close friendship between Cis and Flo was maintained by means of letters, photographs and telephone calls. Flo wrote to say she was returning to England for a visit. Then, at the last minute, this was cancelled because of important developments in her life. She had met and fallen in love with a widower and she was shortly to be married.

The photographs we occasionally receive tell their own story. Flo looks a good ten years younger. She and her husband make each other happy through the love they change. Their first home together was in the Bay of Plenty at a place called Waihi Beach. For her what may have once been only a dream has become a reality, having been confirmed in advance through the signs upon her hands.

CHAPTER 2
Seeing Both Sides

IT cannot be assumed that a woman accompanied by a good-looking man will always find him stimulating. He may sit opposite her, consciously turning his best profile, yet his conversation may turn out to be quite dull. He may on closer acquaintance appear not to be very intelligent. By contrast, a plain-looking man may radiate an inner quality which the same woman would find irresistible. In the presence of the handsome man, time might drag for his audience, whereas in the other's company, an hour could seem like ten minutes.

A woman meeting Paul Metcalf for the first time would feel drawn to him by his appearance, generosity and bonhomie. He would give the impression that she was the only person who mattered to him at that moment and, given the chance, there would be little he would not be prepared to do for her. It was not so much through a natural style or distinctive manner peculiar to himself that Paul attracted attention. It was more noticeably conscious effort in a performance created to impress, and to be turned to his own advantage.

He came to me for a consultation in early summer, on one of those really beautiful days when the sun shines and the birds sing. The image that he projected was that of a strong, virile and sun-tanned outdoor type. I suspected that his easy-going manner was contrived, but I suspended judgment until I had seen his palms.

Parts of the reading which I gave him were good. His career rode on the crest of a wave, with promotion in the offing, and scope for him to cultivate business relationships. Within a few years these could lead to challenging freelance opportunities, and the chance of setting up his own business. Money, property and status were clearly indicated on his hand. Here was a man who could go far. But his emotional and romantic approach to life as seen through palmistic analysis denoted vanity and a shallowness of nature.

During the reading, I sensed that Paul's attitude towards me had changed. From what I had already told him of his nature and work progress, he could not deny that I was for the most part correct in my assessment. I do not think he liked my knowing so much about him. He began to resist. This made no difference to me because I like a challenge and, once I make a statement in a reading with a client, I rarely change it afterwards.

This means that some of my clients are given information which they do not want to accept. I can only hope that whatever I say will be of some benefit to them, even if it only helps them to understand themselves better. Where errors are revealed these are a pointer but not of primary significance. What is important is whether or not the individual concerned can gain wisdom in the period after they have made a mistake, and whether they are able to overcome a weakness in their nature.

Paul's resistance to me did not alter my task. The analysis took a little longer to complete and that was all. My experience of hand-reading convinced me of the need to be neutral, and not to overstate any observations which were necessary in the course of the reading.

Although he was married, his hand told me that he was a womaniser, and that at the time of his visit he was involved in an affair with another woman. I told him so and he did not deny it.

In a hand analysis it is possible to tell the client details relating to other people connected with them. This is because the palm reflects influences of affinity or discord between people who are important to each other.

A double stressful emotional situation was producing conflict for Paul. On one side there was his wife, who loved him and had built her entire world around him. On the other side was 'the other woman'. Unless he pulled himself together and made very careful decisions, the folly of his romantic ambivalence could damage his career as well as cost him dearly financially. My analysis of Paul's situation covered these points. Then time ran out and the consultation ended.

I felt that Paul's future could not be reshaped effectively for him until he personally had dealt with these issues and established in his own mind what he considered were his priorities. Then he could reach decisions on which a fresh outlook on life could be based. Despite his touchiness at the accuracy of my assessment, he may have wanted me to decide for him - to say, 'This is what you should do.' But I cannot do this. Decision-making must always rest with the individual concerned.

Paul came to me only once for a consultation, for reasons which I will explain.

Hidden identity

About three weeks later I was giving a reading to a sensitive, highly-strung but capable woman. Peggy preferred to play a supporting rather than a leading role in life. Her family background and upbringing had been insecure. She was provided for, but that was about all. There was no evidence that she felt loved or understood by her parents, or that she felt she could approach them with any personal problems. Her early experiences had made her a defensive loner.

The turning point for her had been courtship and marriage. Under her husband's influence she lost some of her naivety and developed more self-confidence. She looked upon him as a lover and protector. Had there been a greater age difference between them she might have looked to him as something of a father figure too.

In my analysis I was uneasy because I saw marriage difficulties for her. As gently as I could, I explained this. 'Oh no, you are wrong there,' she told me. 'My marriage is fine. I have no problems there at all.'

'But I am sorry to have to tell you that your marriage is weak, and that there is another woman in your husband's life, now, at this time,' I replied.

She refused to believe that such a thing was possible. I then concentrated on giving her details of the pattern her future was likely to take. This included the prospect of work for herself abroad; and there was an indication of a second marriage, which would provide a comfortable anchorage for her. There was nothing further for me to see for the time being. In any case, she had enough to think about.

The following morning I answered the telephone to hear an irate voice on the attack, without any polite preamble. The speaker was Paul Metcalf. He wanted to know what the devil did I mean by telling his wife that he was having an affair with another woman. He had worked his bile up to such a degree that I had difficulty in getting a word in edgeways.

Calmly, I asked him on what day his wife came to see me. I checked the entries in my appointments diary and read out the surnames, or at least the ones that had been given to me, of all the clients that had been to see me then; Metcalf was not among them. However, he did recognise one of the names that I had mentioned. It transpired that his wife, Peggy, had given her maiden name when making the appointment.

I told Paul that he must credit me with some common-sense and decorum. I pointed out that if a woman of the same surname as his own had sought a consultation after his visit, then I could have reasoned that the two people might be related. Nevertheless, I pointed out, my analysis for the woman would not have altered essentially. I would have told her there was a risk that her husband might be having an affair, rather than confront her with definite information, as I had done. As matters stood there was no way I could reasonably associate the two clients, and they must be prepared to accept the consequences. Our conversation at an end, he rang off, spluttering and somewhat deflated.

An account of the ensuing events was given to me by Peggy when I was able to give her further readings. On the day of Paul Metcalf's phone call to me he went home after work and promptly left the house, telling Peggy that he wanted time to sort himself out. He made no reference to 'the other woman'. He did not tell her where he was going, or for how long. Should it be necessary to pass on an urgent message at any time, she could reach him at his place of business.

Next day Peggy came to see me again, still convinced, in spite of Paul's sudden departure, that her marriage was sound, and that he would soon return. I could only repeat what I had already told her. About a month passed, during which time Paul and Peggy spoke to each other a number of times by telephone, but did not meet. Then Paul phoned his wife to say he would like to meet her and take her out to dinner. Very happy at the prospect of seeing him again, she naturally agreed, and they had a pleasant evening.

After the meal at an exclusive restaurant, he took her back to their home. Peggy's mood was happy, romantic and optimistic. She felt that she was being wooed as in the days of their early courtship, and assumed that her husband was a loving, caring man who would now return home for good, having finally got his thoughts together.

This was not to be. They had not been home for very long when Paul suddenly got angry with Peggy, and with an air of frustration and venom confessed to her, 'Of course I have got another woman; I have been staying with her. We have been having an affair for the last six months. And by the way, I had better phone her now, as she will wonder where I am.' Then immediately, in front of his wife, he dialled the number and talked to his mistress for a full hour.

The truth came as a terrible blow to Peggy. Her naivety, her trust in her man, her belief in their togetherness had been the basis of all her hopes during the period when she had tried to make allowances for his changed attitude and behaviour. Now everything she lived for was being callously shattered in front of her eyes.

She was physically sick and then fainted. Paul stayed with her until she regained consciousness. Then he left her. She followed him outside, running after him, calling to him, yet he ignored her as he got into his car and drove rapidly away into the night.

Having spent a distressing night, crying and sleepless, Peggy went to her job on the following morning. It was no surprise that she couldn't cope with work that day. Her nerves were in a bad state and on one occasion she nearly passed out again. Her colleagues tried to help, offering to take her home, but Peggy refused their assistance. Not in a fit state to work, and intending to go home, she came to see me instead.

A brighter future

When Cis, my lady companion, opened the door to Peggy, she practically fell into her arms and had to be supported to a chair. It took us over two hours of discussion, patience and cups of tea to calm down the distraught woman. She now saw Paul as he really was, and talked of his vanity and selfishness. Eventually, when she could concentrate long enough on what I was telling her, I used hand analysis to explore her future. I predicted a change of job for her, further progress in the field of business which was new to her, and which was connected with travel abroad. This knowledge helped her to pull herself together.

In due course Peggy was offered a retailing job abroad at a good salary. Later she wrote to me giving me the latest news. She had divorced Paul and, as settlement, the house in England was made over to her. Whenever she returned to this country I was able to see her and offer her further guidance and reassurance.

Working abroad and learning another language had transformed Peggy from a broken, down-trodden creature into a confident and organised woman again. It was no surprise to me when she duly announced that she was to marry again. In fun, I reminded her of my earlier prediction in the days when she was married to Paul.

I have now met the new man in her life, who struck me as being a modest, sensible and sincere person. There was none of the handsome womaniser of Paul about him. His eyes were kind and expressive and, although he could not be called handsome, he had a unique charm of his own, and the knack of making others feel at ease in his company. That he could make Peggy happy was evident from their sense of complete harmony which would be strengthened further as time went by. Here was a happy ending.

CHAPTER 3
A Disaster Seen–and Averted

AT such times when I think about my work, I see myself in the role of both observer and helper. During an analysis of a client's situation, I remain mentally detached. My mind must be clear of any impressions before a reading. I won't allow a client's appearance to distract me. In a calm, deliberate manner I look for outstanding features in the hand on which to build my observations.

In my directness I am very careful not to express an opinion. And in the technique I use I do not base a reading on what I think I would do, were I in the client's position. Neither do I push them in any direction. They must use their free-will and choose for themselves which course of action to take out of a number of choices open to them.

I remember a time very early in my career when a woman was brought to me for hand analysis. When examining her hands the first thing I saw was a death sign, with indications that this woman was a potential murderess. For a moment I was completely taken aback and made no comment. I was not sure how to handle the situation. My instinct told me that my interpretation was correct but many years ago, lacking experience, I backed off. I talked about other matters which were important in their way for my client, but in no way compared with the gravity of the terrible feature I had seen: her desire to kill another human being. I did not refer to the subject of death at all. When the reading was completed I said good-bye and watched her leave.

The next few moments were a nightmare of anguish for me. I asked myself if I had done the right thing in ignoring that dreadful sign which I had seen so clearly, and which could have such a terrible effect upon that woman's life. In retrospect those moments of anguish seemed to last for an age, when in reality barely a minute had passed since the woman had left the house.

Having resolved on action, I hurried to the front door, went outside and called the woman back. She returned and I lead her into the room where I had conducted the reading. When she was seated I told her that I had something very important to say, and whether I was right or wrong in doing so, I was determined to tell her what I had seen in her hand, but had left out of the reading.

A potential murderer

It was not a pleasant task. Plainly but gently, I told the woman to her face that she was ready to kill. I described the victim, the weapon - a knife - and both the time and the place of the intended deed. For a second there was silence in the room.

Alma (as I shall call her) stared at me incredulously, her face a pale mask concealing God knows what thoughts at that moment. Then she broke down, sobbing bitterly. Between gasps, shuddering and tears, she began to tell me her story. She had been married for nearly twenty years. Her husband, George, was a successful executive in a big city company. Alma was a few years older than he, and they had no children.

She was a perfectionist. Her home was something of a show piece, of a style that might be featured in a glossy magazine. George provided well for her so that she did not have to go out to work; but she chose to do so. Somewhat temperamental, her moods could change from wishing to do everything at the double, to boredom and frustration. Though she thrived on change, she was often discontented. She tended to over-exert herself to the point of exhaustion, when she would collapse and had to rest.

When other people sometimes paid compliments to her husband, Alma would show displeasure. If other women praised George in her hearing, she would comment, 'You can have him with a bowl of soup.' In this regard, she would ignore semi-serious warnings that if she persisted with this attitude, then some woman would be likely to have designs upon George - soup or no soup.

Then the expected happened. One day, following an argument, George deserted Alma for a young secretary in his office. The anger, bitterness and jealousy which Alma consequently experienced affected her mind. She plotted revenge. She spied on her husband for a fortnight, both at his office and, after some detective work, where he lived with his mistress. Feeling ruthless enough to kill, she even selected the place, the time, and the weapon.

The fates ordained a particular day for the drama. The deed was scheduled to take place in mid-afternoon. But the morning of that very day, a concerned friend paying Alma a visit noticed a strangeness in her behaviour and, feeling that she needed help of some kind, brought the tormented woman to see me.

I could judge from Alma's hand the intensity of her motivation, and the degree of her emotional disturbance. Despite her own faults and mistakes it was clearly indicated that there had been sufficient provocation to justify an alteration in her manner and appearance so far removed from her normal behaviour. As I told her of her propensity to commit murder, I already knew that had she not broken down in front of me and released a tangled web of confused emotion, this woman would have been capable of carrying out her purpose. At the very least her assault upon George would have led to a charge of grievous bodily harm or attempted murder.

Following my dramatic reading, however, Alma made a strong attempt to regain control of her emotions. But there was a very stressful period to follow, during which she made two attempts to take her own life. After each attempt she was saved.

Over the years, I have seen Alma a number of times. I have encouraged her as she learned to accept her situation and to make a new life for herself. George never went back to her, nor did he make any gesture of reconciliation. They have agreed to a legal separation, but have not divorced. It helped in Alma's adjustment that she was able to make new friends, and take up new interests, including a world cruise.

The 'hand map' changes

An interesting aspect of this case was the pattern of lines on the hands. When I first saw Alma's hand and noted the death sign on it, her hands bore only the principal marks: head line, heart line, and life line. The fate and destiny lines were missing. Her hands were also clear of the additional fine lines which are usually to be found on the average person's palms.

Curiously, during the years since then, both of Alma's hands have developed many other lines, including the fate line which commenced in its form somewhat high on the palm. The other new lines have formed chiefly in areas of the palm where they are commonly found. Alma's hand markings now relate to her actions, and vice versa. This is an example of a direct link being established between the subconscious, the conscious mind and memory, and the ensuing projection of an individual's future.

Incidentally, there is no guarantee that the reader of this page will live through the next five seconds! A bizarre thought, you might think. However, whether or not anyone will live through the next five seconds is determined by a Higher Power, the God-force. On the basis that a person can and does survive the next five seconds, then for that individual there is a future to be experienced and something to be made from it.

CHAPTER 4
Cautious Optimism

ALTHOUGH they may not necessarily be sceptics, some of the people that come to see me are more cautious at the very least. I will quote you an example. My telephone rings; the caller wishes to make an appointment. When I ask for a name for the booking, the caller says, 'Do I have to give you my name?' And I reply, 'Well, give me a name - any name will do, so long as you know who you are when you come to see me.'

I acknowledge the need for some people to remain anonymous in various situations. I know a learned and respected author who began his writing career anonymously as the creator of at least two erotic, if not obscene, novels. Some means justify the end! But I am puzzled as to why a client should be afraid to give me his or her name. Are they, I ask myself, not prepared to be themselves? Upon enquiry, I learn that some folk are anxious at having to wait up to six weeks for a consultation with me. They imagine that during the interval I am busy checking them out somehow, unearthing and exposing facts about their origin, background and circumstances. Yet had I the time to do so, I would not even bother myself with such an escapade.

There are, however, variations upon a theme. My telephone rang. The caller, a women, wished to make an appointment. The day and time being decided, she then asked, 'Do you want me to give you my London name, or would you prefer to have my other name?' For a moment I wondered what type of London name would apply, and then said she could give me any name she wished. I smiled as I wrote her appointment in my diary, and wondered what my secretive client would be like.

However much I may feel that I understand part of the pattern of human behaviour, in my work there is always something fresh coming to light, new knowledge about people and how they live their lives. For the most part I find it absorbing, interesting, challenging and fruitful. The good that can be seen to be done for others through my work, far outweighs the small areas of frustration I occasionally encounter.

Believing the good news

Some people are reluctant to accept good news readily. For example, there was the instance when I told the client he would win a reasonable amount of money. His reaction was to laugh and say, 'You are wrong there. I am not lucky: I never win anything.' My reply was, 'If that is how you feel, you have said it aloud now and convinced yourself that this is so. You are no longer positive because you have sent the good that it represents away from you.'

Had I told this man something of not a particularly happy nature, according to his mode of thinking he would have been more prepared to accept what was to come. It appears that such people are drawn to that which is morbid. They willingly tell you of their woes and tribulations. You seldom hear them recount a happy experience. It is almost as though their lives do not justify happy or pleasurable experiences.

I like being able to forecast pleasant omens for people whenever possible; not that I am one to cajole, but it is clearly rewarding to see something agreeable or delightful and describe it. A woman who was disillusioned and low-spirited because of a broken romance, would not accept my prediction that she would marry for a second time; her partner would be a man much older than herself; he would be wealthy and would take her to live abroad in his home country. Again this was one of those cases where I learned about the sequel to the consultation from another person entirely. I couldn't help wondering how this once disillusioned woman felt when, within a year of my predictions, she was courted by an older man whom she married, after which they made their home in Italy.

Traditionally, palmistry carries with it an aura of fascination, mystery and fear. Two contrasting attitudes to this ancient, natural science are illustrated in the following account.

When not engaged in my profession or lecturing I like nothing better than to share a relaxing atmosphere with some close friends. Three of us decided to go for a drive in the country at a leisurely pace, enjoying the open air and the scenic beauty of a late summer afternoon. We stopped for tea in a quaint country village. Cakes and tea refreshed us.

A tea-time reading

The room in which we sat was cool and restful. The lazily measured tick of an elaborately inlaid longcase clock encouraged us to take our time in that peaceful setting. We were the only customers in the place.

The waitress who came to our table had an air of elegant refinement. She had an interesting face with a high intelligent forehead and alert eyes which concealed kindness, until she smiled. Instinctively I thought of her as a loner who had not had an easy life. She wore no ring on her hand. I supposed she was not married. Seeing to our needs, she entered into light conversation with us.

Looking directly at me she said she thought I was a teacher. My lady companion, Cis, smilingly told her that this was not so, but the other member of the trio was. Cis followed this up by asking the waitress, 'Would you like to know what work he does?'

'Yes.' 'He is a palmist.' Immediately the waitress became enthusiastic, held out both of her hands to me, and asked me to tell her what I saw there. I am not often prepared to work on my day off but I entered into the spirit of the thing and made a short analysis of her personality and character, after which I made a couple of future forecasts for her.

At this point a women's head appeared round an adjoining door. Her eyes opened wide for some seconds as she listened. I later learned that this women was the waitress' elder sister. Her hair was pulled severely up to the back of her head, and she wore little make-up as far as I could tell. Seeing what was happening, she admonished her sister in clear tones.

'You don't want to have that done,' she said, 'it will turn your brain.' Whereupon she promptly disappeared, and those of us in the lounge had a good laugh. A minute or so later, out of sight, the women called again to her sister, 'You are wanted in the kitchen.' Our waitress hurried off, but after a short time reappeared for the completion of her hand analysis.

Within years the premises were sold, and our waitress moved on to the next stage towards a new life which opened up before her, as was predicted. The story of the second part of my prediction to her was yet to come.

CHAPTER 5
The Pursuit of Happiness

WHATEVER the manner of people's lives throughout the world, they all have a common goal - the hope to experience happiness. Whether they find it, and having done so whether they can hold on to it, depends not only on themselves but on countless outside influences, a chequer board of ifs and yeas and nays.

The capacity for enjoyment, for sharing pleasure with others of like mind, is a gift to be treasured and a source of contentment. The fortunate possessor has achieved one of the principal aims of life. At this point his or her search for happiness may cease as desire becomes limited by present enjoyment. Having some comforts at hand can make the problems met in a lifetime that much easier to bear. And from the whole experience a precious wisdom can be gathered, which says simply: live for now. The Biblical phrase is apt which says, 'sufficient unto the day thereof...'

For some people, however, the pursuit of happiness is far from straightforward. The reason for this is not always clear or easy to accept. An ancient law of nature tells us that we earn whatever befalls us in life, be it for good or ill, brought about by our own actions or otherwise. Should happiness elude us, it is because a price has to be paid in terms of self-sacrifice or a personal test, whatever its nature.

When Sylvia Lane first came to me for a consultation she displayed nervousness, doubt and fear. Her highly-strung nature made her impatient to find a solution to her problems. She wanted next year's answers yesterday! In a preliminary examination of her hand I could see no immediate end to the strain she was enduring.

Regardless of her willpower she had reached a point in her life where she was a victim of circumstances.

Sylvia was an attractive and intelligent married woman. She had a good dress sense, kept up to date with fashion and knew how to show her figure to best advantage. In a good mood, her love of life could be appealing and infectious, but occasionally her eyes expressed tension and a sense of defeat.

After some years of marriage, she admitted to herself that she no longer loved her husband. On reflection she also realised that her husband was not her true choice of partner. She had allowed him to claim her, and her own lack of choice was confirmed by the line markings on her hand. For his part, her husband had a jealous and possessive nature. He controlled the marriage, overpowered it, you might say, by a combination of ambition for success, selfishness and an urge to dominate. This situation affected Sylvia to the extent that it made her react as a secondary person, keeping her 'in her place' and stifling her initiative. If she said anything against her husband, she was punished for it. His kindness could turn to cruelty in an instant.

A second chance

He owned and controlled an expanding leisure goods business. Sylvia was given the job of running the thriving export department. Then in her thirties she met a younger, single man in the course of the work, and they embarked on a love affair.

Having rejected earlier opportunities to be unfaithful, Sylvia now found herself deeply in love, with an intensity of feeling she had never before believed possible. When the affair had continued for some months, she asked her husband for a divorce, without mentioning the other man in her life.

Her husband suspected that she might have a lover, but he was unable to prove it. He refused point blank to give her her freedom and, true to type, began to humiliate and degrade her in front of others, as well as when they were alone together. At the same time, he became more insistent in his demands for conjugal rights.

Sylvia had no money of her own. She did not wish to involve her parents in her dilemma, and inevitably she began to feel more and more trapped. Her only hope was that her lover could help her escape from her husband, and that they could eventually make a new life together.

In my analysis, based on examination of her palms, I could see her love affair continuing and strengthening over the next five years. But some severe obstacles would have to be overcome, before this relationship could stand a chance of leading to permanent happiness.

Every gesture a person makes is an expression of free-will; this is a factor which always has to be considered. Opportunities can present themselves but the individual may not always choose to avail of them. On the other side, as in Sylvia's case, external circumstances can be the deciding factor. I could forsee an end to her love affair, not necessarily because she and her lover wished it so, but through outside influences.

Long-term forecasts are often built up from short-term possibilities which, linked together, produce a main theme. I could see how important it was for Sylvia to pursue her hopes. But while explaining this I stressed the difficulties ahead in a long drawn-out divorce case, as her husband was still adamant that he would not give her her freedom.

'I don't believe in coincidence'

Sylvia came for several consultations, and it was during an interval between her visits that destiny intervened in an unexpected fashion. I don't believe in coincidence; events happen or they do not. What followed was meant to happen.

Another client, having no connection whatever with Sylvia, came to see me for advice on business matters. An ambitious businessman, self-taught, shrewd and alert, he was a natural survivor who chose to work on a sub-contractual or self-employed basis rather than risk being at a disadvantage in working for someone else.

Two business propositions were open to my client. I saw that the first was a speculative short-term venture which would involve him with an associate whom I saw as a weak link in the working arrangement. I advised him to explore one contract only with this associate initially, and then to seek other contracts on more agreeable terms. Clearly, this man was a sore point in my client's affairs. He commented as follows:

'I know this associate. I have put business his way and he owes me a fair amount of money already. He thinks he is sharp and that he is getting one over on me. I am tempted to take action, but there is no need to, for he will get his come-uppance from somebody else. He is knocking off the wife of a man who runs a local business, but who had contacts with the underworld, so together they will 'sort him out'. They were talking about this in the pub the other night.'

So it came about that Sylvia and her lover were named to me by a third party, who was ignorant of the fact that she was one of my clients, too. Despite having this unexpected information, I felt I had to keep an open mind while examining Sylvia's case. When in due course she visited me again, I wanted to see what information her hand offered, rather than allow my reading to be influenced by what I had heard.

On this occasion, Sylvia was tired, run-down and anxious. I said I could see that meetings with her lover were difficult to arrange because of her husband's suspicions. Despite the fact that she was in love, her affair was likely to end soon. At this point she began to weep and then told me about her difficulties. Yes, her husband was suspicious. He had tried to catch her out on a number of occasions. Eventually he said he knew where her lover lived, and that two of his pals were going to sort out 'lover boy'.

As soon as she could, Sylvia telephoned to warn her lover. But, foolishly, she used the telephone in her office, and her husband overheard her conversation. On a separate line he telephoned his 'pals' to send them on a mission. Later, he told his wife sarcastically, 'He won't get away you know,' and smiled at her misery.

It was afternoon. For hours he did not let Sylvia out of his sight, insisting that she remain with him, although that was the last thing she wanted to do at that time. Later, the telephone rang and her husband answered. It was one of his pals to say they had gone to a certain address but that the bird had flown. From papers they found there they deduced that their quarry had headed off at full speed for Dover. One of the accomplices set off in pursuit while the other stayed at the house in case their prey returned.

Later that same day another telephone call came through to Sylvia's husband. The hunter had located her lover's car, which had been left in a car park in Dover. They had arrived too late to prevent him from boarding the hovercraft which would reach France within an hour. The husband's response was to make another telephone call, this time to France, to arrange a reception committee for the young man on his arrival.

These events happened over two years ago. Nothing has been heard of Sylvia's lover since the day he left these shores. He disappeared, apparently without trace, and it can be assumed that he is still listed as a 'missing person'. Sylvia did not obtain a divorce from her husband. Surprisingly she has remained with him in his enterprise, and business continues as usual.

CHAPTER 6
Personal Failings

A SMALL percentage of my case histories tell of failure for one reason or another. A person who is obstinate, narrow-minded and unimaginative may need help with some problems, but nevertheless will not accept solutions designed to solve the problems once and for all. A contradiction of terms can arise as, for example, when a person is seeking an alternative aim of purpose in life in contrast to his customary life-style. Beneficial changes may be on offer, yet those affected resist them, remaining victims of their situation. Or they may complicate the issue further by continual indecision.

There are people who thrive on complication and an unsettled way of life. Their lives would be empty were it not for the drama associated with constant disruption of routine. I know of a once-married woman who could not recover from the humiliation and bitterness of divorce, but who subsequently used her considerable physical charms to attract the attentions of men. Apparently each man in turn was prepared to love her, whereas she had not the slightest inclination of giving her love to anyone. Furthermore, she chose to attract only men who had secure marriages themselves. When matters reached a pitch where the man involved took steps to break from his wife and children for her sake, then the seductress would end the relationship in an ugly fashion.

There was a time when a certain woman used to visit me frequently, always arriving unannounced, and almost pleading for help. On one occasion she saw me in the street, whereupon she ran excitedly towards me, arms spread wide, her hair streaming in the wind. Yet I was never sure if she really listened to my reading.

Unhappily married, she just wanted someone to hold her hand and talk to her (while her husband waited in his car, incidentally). I felt that if I had quoted stock exchange prices or washing instructions from a detergent packet, it would not have made the slightest difference, because she was lost in a fantasy world of her own creation. But in reality she also knew that life could offer her nothing better than the security she already had in her present marriage.

It is essential for me to keep an open mind at all times. Although strictly neutral, during the reading I am involved in my client's world, to observe and assess, but never to judge. However familiar clients may be with their circumstances and what they believe are the choices open to them, their view tends to be limited. As an observer and consultant, I have a broader perspective. My work often enables me to point out possible solutions which had not occurred to them. But while I may suggest that a new direction might be more beneficial, I never make decisions for clients. I believe that they must decide for themselves what they can do, supported by advice and encouragement.

Occasionally, however, I encounter a condition affecting a client which is so tormented, confused and complicated that counselling is more difficult than usual. From the onset, there is no clear indication that the client can ever cure himself of this malady, however many chances are given. Such clients are recognised by a discernible aura of unrest and disorder. This is more obvious in some cases. Those affected have a haunted look, and an intensity which works against themselves instead of being used constructively for their own good.

If this emotional intensity is akin to magnetism - and electromagnetism plays a part in life - the situation is rather like positive meeting positive, resulting in repulsion. My suggestions as to changes which would help such clients may be correct, but something in their own make-up compels them to stay as they are, thus adding to their present suffering.

Such a person was Brenda Cawston. Young, good looking, with more energy than she knew how to handle at times, she lived in a limited world of her own making. Through a mixture of habit, intention, and lack of personal discipline, she drew others to her and used them. When she got what she wanted, she could be charming: but if she could not get her own way, or things went wrong for her, she was transformed into an erratic, unreasonable and unmanageable being.

When I first looked at the lines on her palms, I thought the pattern presented was a mess. Although there were different line markings on each of her hands, the overall picture reflected inherent confusion as to who she was and who she was trying to be. I counted up the children marks visible on one of her hands, and saw that she was capable of having a large family. She should by then have had twelve children! In fact, she had already had several miscarriages, and three successful pregnancies.

Part-time mother

Brenda's children were not living with her at that time. They lived with other people for short periods, thus giving her the peculiar status of part-time mother. During my first reading I saw from her hands that her husband could be vicious towards her and that her marriage was not at all secure. I warned her that if she went back to her husband, she could be taking her life in her hands. I advised her to keep away from him and to be prepared for divorce. Brenda was pregnant again at the time, which did not help matters, yet I had to make a stand on the indications I saw on her palms. There was no doubt in my mind the prediction was accurate.

Brenda disregarded my advice. Within three weeks she had returned without an appointment, needing help desperately. She had been beaten up severely. Her face was bruised; her nose broken. And she had lost her baby. She had gone back to live with her husband. One day a ferocious argument had broken out between them, during which her husband lost control of himself. He subsequently went to prison, having been found guilty of causing her grievous bodily harm, and it was on these grounds that she later obtained a divorce.

I saw Brenda frequently. With each successive analysis I hoped that she would have learnt from her past mistakes. In relatively short time she chose a lover, and brought him to see me. At that particular analysis, I could see a troubled future in store for both of them. Brenda was pregnant again, being one of those women who conceived very easily. I foresaw, too, the probable loss of the baby at childbirth. She simply was not physically fit enough for another pregnancy at the time. How could I tell her that she would lose this baby, too? I was reasonably certain that this would happen. When she asked me how the child would be, I replied that her stamina was poor, and that she would need a blood transfusion after delivery. Circumstances then took Brenda and her husband-to-be elsewhere. I must admit that I was somewhat relieved to see her go, despite the experience her case had given me. Later, one of her colleagues told me that Brenda had lost her baby at birth. She was still with her man, but their way of life continued to be beset by complications.

Everyone plays a part in creating a harmonious or disruptive environment for themselves. If you were to eat indiscriminately at one sitting, you would incur the risk of indigestion, in which case the trouble would be of your own making. On the other hand, you can adopt a different approach in your selection of food and ask yourself, 'Do I want this mixture to become part of me?' If you decide not to over-indulge your appetite, you will know that you have chosen wisely.

The ability to resist too wide a choice is a clear indicator of emotional maturity. 'As we think, so we are' is no less true when applied to palmistry. The lines upon the hand indicate a person's potential, that which is in store for them here and now, but they also point to the choices ahead and the manner of the person's response to them.

Learning the hard way

One day my telephone was out of order, so I called the telecommunications engineers to put it right. Two men arrived, and it occurred to me that the younger one must be an apprentice. They both expressed curiosity about my profession but said they did not believe that palmistry was beneficial to the public. The younger man showed me his hands, and in a few sentences I described his character, personality and general potential for the immediate future. I added that I thought it advisable for him to avoid an early marriage, as he was not mature enough to take on responsibilities of the kind marriage involved. Consequently, a too-early marriage could lead to divorce.

Upon hearing this, the young man flushed with embarrassment. 'But I'm getting married in a fortnight,' he said. His workmate could not quite suppress a stifled guffaw. I re-examined his hands and told him that I would not alter a word of my prediction. I then left them to get on with their work, and my telephone was duly repaired.

Within eighteen months, I was giving a reading to an attractive young woman with a fresh complexion and long blonde hair. I discussed her marriage problems, and the prospects of legal separation and divorce, after which I described the scope of a new future open to her and leading towards a second marriage. On completion of the reading, she told me who she was.

Her husband was the young telephone engineer. I was proved right about his inability to cope with the responsibilities of marriage, and in my prediction that his wife would be provoked into seeking first a legal separation and then a divorce. He had become an early loser, believing more in fantasy than reality, and a practical-minded woman had taught him a very sharp lesson. Although I have not seen him since that first and only meeting, I have twice met his older workmate, who on both occasions gave me a knowing nod. A cautious man given to few words, his one comment was,'I shall never again doubt the authenticity of palmistry.'

The theme of as you think, so you are' can be broadened to suit other situations, as in the case of romantic infatuation or romantic over-possessiveness. Not only can this result in unnecessary complications, but it can somtimes lead to years of wasted effort for those involved.

It used to be a pleasure to meet Michael Phelps when he first came to see me some years ago. He then had a striking personality, which manifested itself in the enjoyment of life. Intelligent and resourceful, he would enthusiastically discuss his realistic ambitions for the future. He was a first-rate pilot and flying was his life. Of all the women he could have chosen, destiny had placed in his path a girl who had experienced a disruptive home life. Her upbringing had shaped her nature in such a way as to make her feelings alternate between high and low, from hot to cold. The vicious undercurrent in her emotional make-up made her incapable of deep feelings for anyone. And to compensate she would indulge in a charade of elaborate pretence, deceiving Michael into believing that he was winning her love, which in fact did not exist.

Over a long period I saw the change and decline wrought in Michael by this situation. As a palmist I saw the line markings upon his hands change position; for line markings on the palmar surface are not fixed from birth to death as is popularly supposed. Michael had become the victim of that most painful malady, unrequited love. He became unfit to fly, and had to give up the career he loved. He refused to admit that the woman did not love him, and eventually she left him for another man who could provide her with a better standard of living.

I saw all this on Michael's hand before the woman came into his life, and I saw it even more clearly in the early stages of their relationship. I as the consultant and he as the client needing help and guidance, pulled in opposite directions. When I told him frankly that he should terminate the relationship, he clung to her all the more, determined to win her over.

I looked at her palms. Each palm was covered with a maze of lines. If you said to her, 'I have an apple and an orange. That is all I can offer you, so which do you want?' she would ask instead for a banana.

Michael has often been very close to nervous breakdown. His self-made torment continues. He wants the woman back. Although on a number of occasions he tried to establish a relationship with someone else, that inexplicable flaw in his emotional nature still leads him to persevere in the false hope that one day he will be reunited with the love of his life. I can do nothing for him now (he knows this very well) until he is ready to accept the healing change which comes from within himself.

Uncertain future

Love can be called an affection of the mind by that which delights, whereas passion is a powerful feeling of pain or suffering linked to the agitation of the mind through an ardent love which impresses the soul. In the case of another of my clients, Joy Dickinson, passion meant great suffering when she allowed herself to fall in love with William Lambert.

Joy had been married many years to a husband with whom she had little in common. There were two children of the marriage who, in turn, were married and living their own lives by the time Joy first came to see me. Once her children had left home, the marriage weakened further. Then to make something of her life, and as a gesture of independence, Joy got a job in an employment agency. Her job also served as a distraction from her emotional doubts and loneliness at this stage, since she and her husband seldom went out together as a couple, preferring instead to mix with the company of others.

Thus Joy met William Lambert, who together with his wife made a sociable foursome. Ironically the Lamberts' marriage was in as bad a state as her own. Because they were both lonely and felt that they were misunderstood, Joy and William found solace in each other's company and were soon involved in an affair.

This love affair was clearly visible in Joy's hand when she first visited me. In assessing her situation I could see that it had been going on for many years, and showed every sign of continuing. What I could not see clearly was whether or not she would always be happy with William. Her hand showed that she felt strongly about him; but it also showed areas of uncertainty on her future.

In palmistry, there is a feature which I call 'hand speed' which falls into three classes or orders. Take, for example, an alert, ambitious and capable business person used to making rapid decisions in both home and business life. This person's hand would relate to his nature where progress could be calculated in terms of being able to create opportunities compatible with environmental conditions. Such a person's circumstances would seldom be static or stagnant. The pattern of changes would be shown in the line markings of the palms, as would the capacity to respond quickly and decisively to an opportunity put before them. This could be termed a 'fast hand'.

In contrast, in the case of a cautious-minded person accustomed to a life of straightforward, unchanging routine the palms would display through the line markings the symptoms of a 'slow hand'. One year in this person's life would not be much different from another.

(See pages 53, 54 and 55 for examples of hand speeds).

Joy Dickinson's hand was of the slow type . I was uneasy for her, because during my analysis I felt that it would take a considerable time for circumstances to change to be of lasting benefit to her. Though she seemed happy to an extent,her palm signs showed that she was experiencing the uncertainties of a'limbo' situation. Each subsequent analysis involved repetition of earlier forecasts. Change could not be speeded up in any direction. As an observer I could only watch and wait for improvements.

Eventually the time came when Joy and William convinced themselves that it would be absurd for them to lead separate lives, when they could be happy together. They planned to desert their respective marriage partners once William, who was some years older than Joy, retired from work.

At last the waiting was over and they were able to implement their plan. They set up home together in a rented house further south. Joy gave up her job and her pension was frozen. Like any newly-wed couple they were blissfully happy as they set about furnishing their new home.

Within eight weeks and without any warning, William announced his intention to return to his wife. Behind the scenes, she had kept in touch with him and kept pressing him to go back to her. He did so, leaving Joy distraught and bewildered, high and dry. This was an almost unbearably unhappy time for her. William kept in touch, telephoning her regularly, and promising that he would come back to her. He kept his promise, and left his wife for a second time. Overjoyed at having him back with her, Joy forgot the pain of their earlier parting. All was well again. The sun shone and the birds sang.

To celebrate their reunion she suggested that they should have a holiday abroad, and he readily agreed. So with her usual efficiency, she made all the arrangements. In her new-found happiness she felt years younger.

The day before they were due to fly off, William produced another bombshell. He left Joy for the second time, telling her to go ahead and enjoy her holiday nevertheless. And yes, he would be in touch when she returned.

It would be an understatement to say that in this situation Joy could not think straight. Numbed by events she decided to go on holiday after all. But, not surprisingly, she did not enjoy a moment of it. On her return she waited in vain for William to contact her. Time passed and she still waited. Eventually she heard from a mutual acquaintance that he had died. As if there were not enough sadness in her life already, more was to come, for three months after William's death Joy's own husband died.

Her financial position, never very strong, deteriorated further. Because she had not reached retirement age her pension remained frozen. She could no longer afford to pay the rent for the home they had shared, and in which she was still living. Somehow, her will-power sustained her. By adapting her life-style to her changed circumstances, Joy was able to obtain work with a family, and an unfurnished flat went with the job. To this day she still carries a torch for William Lambert.

The slow hand speed

This representative style of hand is inclined to be large with little suppleness. Line forms are simple, comprising four principal lines: Head line, Heart line, Life line and Fate or Destiny line, with little showing of ancillary lines. Lines which are visible are mainly large,

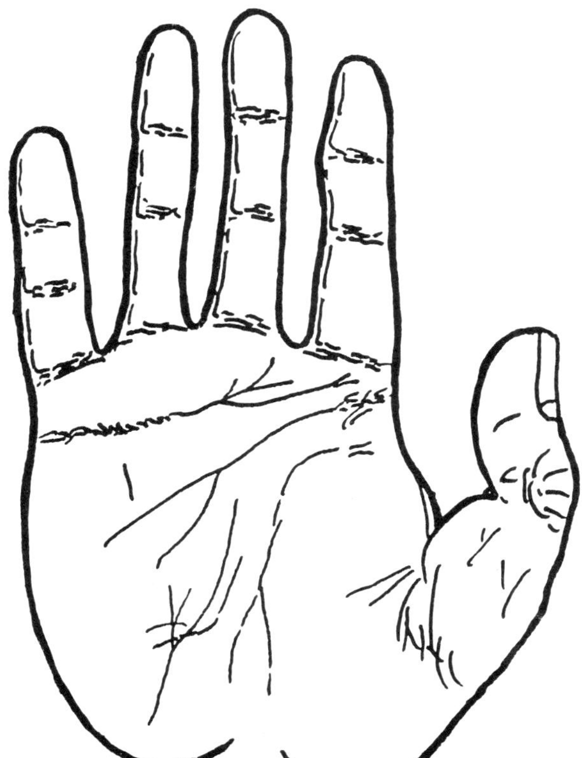

Hand Speed: An example of the'slow hand'

tend to be deep set and to traverse horizontally. Observe how the finger shape emerges as somewhat stiff, short in length, broad and square-cut in appearance. The finger-tips are short, the fingernails are broad. The thumb is noticeable on account of its being unusually strong and well developed.

The temperament of the 'slow hand' person shows him or her as being usually quiet and reserved, benevolent in attitude, and for the most part of steady equilibrium. However, this latter tendency can be undermined to a considerable extent in situations involving strong emotion. This person tends to be of average intelligence,

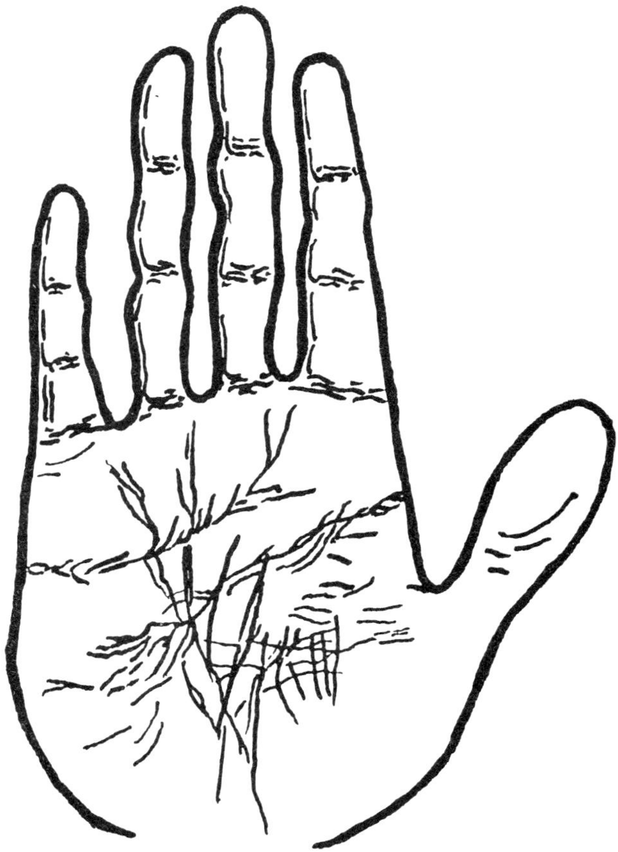

Hand Speed: An example of a 'medium-paced hand'

cautious and having a good memory. They are often methodical and painstaking in what they choose to do, display both determination and obstinacy, and are inclined to display intuition and to be superstitious.

The medium-paced hand

This style of hand is of the bony type. The palm tends to be stiff, or offers a resistance of its own, yet the fingers are long and flexible, and can easily be bent backwards. In some instances the little finger tends to be short. Fingernails are short or narrow. Across

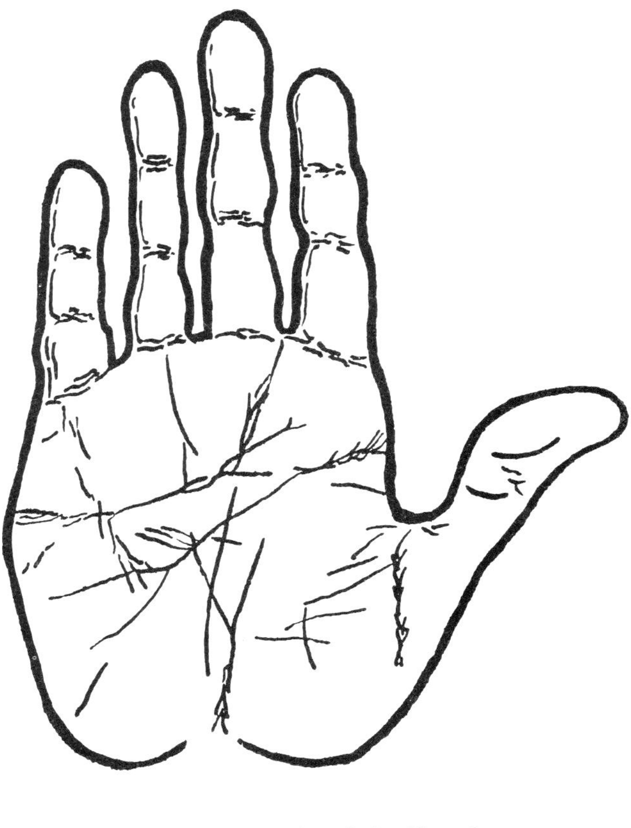

Hand Speed: An example of the 'fast hand'

the palmar surface many fine ancillary lines can be seen.

Persons with such hands are likely to be highly sensitive, with a continually active mind and nervous system. Outwardly they display vitality and creative energy. Although they show a strong interest in active life, they are likely to seek refuge in nature. Artistic and exuding charm, humour and warmth towards others, they are given to contemplation, nevertheless, and to withdrawing at times into a world of their own.

It can be ascertained palmistically that such a person has a tendency to evade responsibilities due to a self- made fear affecting self-confidence; they would worry that certain responsibilities could become overbearing. Due to weakness of will-power this person is not a true decision maker, but is of the type to submit himself to destiny. Aided sometimes by intuition, so that his strategy doesn't seem such a gamble, he allows chance to intervene.

The fast hand speed

This hand is flexible sensitive and broad. The fingers are fleshy and tend to be of medium length. The fingernails are filbert in style, but in most instances they are broad and of medium length. The thumb is strong, well formed and powerful in appearance.

The owner of this type of hand is a natural extrovert. He or she is a realist, an organiser, someone who accepts responsibility easily and well, thriving on challenges to intellect and ability. The person has immeasurable strength of purpose, high ideals and a stong driving force. Behind a calm and stable temperament, there is a sense of dedication to various causes and a determination to express strong ideals.

Although undoubtedly strong minded, this person is not necessarily self assertive. A methodical thinker, observer and analyst, he or she can be most self-critical in considering personal achievement and might be described as a fanatic. Certainly there is a tendency to be reactionary if opposed, or where personal ambition is obstructed for some reason. But in such an event he would quickly discover another path to success.

Self-inflicted wounds

Self-destructive influences lurk within some personalities as if they are bound to re-enact some Greek tragedy. Such persons seem irresistibly drawn to drama, as without it their lives would lack colour and purpose. But it is not always possible to discover whether these self-inflicted wounds bring them comfort. They can appear indifferent to the havoc they create for those closest to them. They may challenge Fate to take a kick at them and, given licence, it will. Cosmically and spiritually, they may feel compelled to take that self-destructive course, so that the malady can work its way out of the system, and atonement can follow.

No-one knows for certain how the line markings came to be formed upon the human palm. These have nothing to do with the muscle and tendon structures of the hand. The Old Testament, (Book of Job, chapter 37) says: 'God thundereth marvellously with his voice; great things doeth He which we cannot comprehend.' Verse 7 reads: 'He sealeth up the hand of every man; that all men may know his work.' In the original Hebrew of the Book of Job (chapter 37, verse 7) we find these significant words: 'God caused signs or seals on the hands of all the sons of men, that the sons of men might know their works.'

I believe the markings on the palm to be the interaction between the spiritual and physical zones within the life force. This in turn is related to man's dual consciousness, his subjective mind and his objective mind. Each individual born has the task of maintaining a balance between the two; they are after all a composition of spirit and matter. Whether we believe in a God-force or not is a choice left open to us. The believer adapts to a faith, perhaps a religion. Atheists and agnostics who doubt that man is made from a blending of spirit with matter, put themselves in the strange position of denying their own existence, because were it not for the working of spirit they would not be here.

Religion is an interpretation of a spiritual truth or law which, in turn, is governed to some degree by geographical environment. A person born in Tibet may become a Buddhist; a person born in Saudi Arabia may become a follower of Islam; in Ireland the choice might be between Catholic and Protestant. Yet an individual may not subscribe to any of these faiths, but could persue his own doctrine and beliefs whether they be right or wrong.

Persons who are self-destructive can, rightly or wrongly, incorporate in their life pattern their own mental or emotional *hari-kari* . If this is predestined for them, this is something they may have to go through. I would like to share with you the case of

Mrs Angela Plowright, to illustrate this argument.

I met Anglea through George Grimble, who brought her along when he came to me for a consultation. In appearance George looked like a yeoman farmer of a bygone age, a steady old boy in pace and manner of the type described by country people as 'the salt of the earth.'

His hands were rather large, work-worn and weather-worn. The principal lines upon them traversed the palms, leaving other areas of the hand relatively open, with few minor fine ancillary marks. I saw portrayed in his hands a natural cautiousness, counter-balanced by a stubborn capacity, trends increasingly emphasised after a first marriage ending in the palmistic symbol of divorce. I could see the patterns indicating the prospect of business developments, some choice of domestic re-adjustment and the possibility of a second marriage.

When I looked at Angela's palms, what struck me as the most significant was her life-long concern with security, which elicited from her an intuitive response aimed at self-preservation. The areas of the her hand reflecting romantic nature and emotional range displayed a complicated and moody temperament, forever restless, searching, suggesting contentment to be an illusion for her.

Physically, she was a striking woman with expressive eyes. She had a beautiful skin enhanced by a natural bloom , and a dress sense which resulted in up-to-the-minute elegance. She was used to people taking notice of her, but concealed her pleasure in their approval behind a carefully contrived mixture of warmth and inaccessibility.

Over a period of time I had many opportunities to observe George and Angela, both together and separately. With each consultation I gave them in turn, it became more of a challenge for me to remain a neutral observer. I could see the plot take shape two ways, firstly in the direction of their development as individuals, and secondly in terms of their joint progress. This became an interesting study. It was like watching a chess game between two players, in which harmony and lack of unity operated side by side, yet on different planes - a contradictory pattern of behaviour needing to be worked out by the couple themselves.

George Grimble was a self-employed man who, helped by his son, ran a business involved in the sale and maintenance of second-hand equipment. After his divorce he had decided to live on his own, remaining largely independent. He met Angela Plowright through his business connection with her mother, and learned that she had been divorced some years earlier and had one child. Since then she lived with her mother, neglecting to cultivate any form of social life for herself, so that she had become something of a recluse. As their friendship grew, Angela began to show an interest in George's work, much to the approval of her mother. The age difference between them was considerable, yet this did not seem to matter to them.

One day George asked Angela what she would like to do with her life. Now more self-confident, she told him that she had one cherished wish - to run a restaurant. Luckily George was in a position to buy premises which could be converted to her requirements, and very soon she was established as a restaurant manageress. Shortly after this, they began to live together.

However, it was soon apparent that the restaurant was not doing well financially. Initially, Angela had tried her best to make a success of the business opportunity created for her, but she had now become disenchanted with the enterprise, as though her enthusiasm for the restaurant had burnt itself out. The outcome was that the property and business had eventually to be sold.

More and more frequently in the readings which followed, I detected an irritating undercurrent of discord in both of their lives. The reaction was more clearly shown in George's hand, giving the impression that he wanted more personal recognition from Angela, and that this was promised after a fashion, but never fulfilled. Angela's own palms continued to register concern for security, which emerged as her priority, whereas her romantic feelings towards George remained subdued. Conversely, his practical endeavours were increasingly influenced by his desire to win Angela's love. While I could foresee the continuation of a trial marriage relationship for him, from my readings of his hand I could not guarantee that the two of them would ever achieve a lasting harmony. This opinion was reinforced by her hand at the corresponding period, which indicated emotional withdrawal from their relationship.

Consequently, I felt compelled to advise George that it would not be sensible to marry her. Instead, he should accept the level of mutual happiness that could be achieved through their continuing to live together. This was the message registered on both their hands, defining their relationship simply as an extended affair of the heart. I do not think he believed me at the time, because he did not wish to believe me. And, no doubt, he hoped to prove me wrong. He continued his campaign to win her. They moved to a Tudor-style property in its own grounds, and outwardly they appeared a happy couple.

The affair of the heart had lasted for approximately sixteen years when, during one of her solo visits to me, and perhaps detecting that I was self-conscious about their relationship, Angela told me that she and George had married. Remembering my advice to George, my instant reaction was recoil, which I did my best to conceal. My personal discipline required that as a consultant I must remain neutral towards my clients. Yet I could still see this commitment leading to the destruction of such harmony as existed between the couple, just as I had forecast earlier. Outwardly I offered them both my congratulations and best wishes.

Less than twenty months later, George came to see me. One did not need to look at his hands to see what was wrong. It was written only too clearly on his face. During an argument Angela had suddenly told him of her intention to obtain a divorce. Once the words were said it appeared that there was no hope of retraction. It was a sadder, wiser man who looked me in the eye and told me that as soon as his wife had spoken, he recalled my words to him: 'It would be better for you, emotionally, romantically and financially, if you were to live with Angela rather than marry her.' The last act of this modern tragedy had been played.

CHAPTER 7
The Powers of Reason

WHAT do we mean by instinct and intuition? Let us look at it this way. If you take away reason and experience from our thought processes, you are left with instinct, which allows you to function on only one level of consciousness. But if instinct can be intensified so that your consciousness is activated to function on a higher level, then you have a state of enhanced mental awareness where the truth of things can be perceived without reasoning or analysis. This is what is meant by intuition.

If you further enhance this state of awareness with the addition of spiritual qualities, then you enter into the realm of psychic vision. These different levels of consciousness can only be fully understood if a person's mind has evolved sufficiently. It is not enough merely to be aware that these different levels can be attained. They must be experienced if they are to be properly evaluated. Common sense can challenge intelligence. Intelligence without common sense is an over-developed faculty.

I once had a very dear friend who could solve any mathematical problem, however complex. Furthermore, he could demonstrate two or three methods by which the correct answer could be obtained. Yet this same man, despite his science degree, couldn't repair a fuse. In simple domestic matters he was quite helpless and, no matter how hard he tried, the fuse remained unrepaired, and all he had to show for his effort was a lost temper.

Ideally a balance should be maintained between a realistic mental attitude and the intuitive levels within the subconscious part of the mind. At most stages in life, human beings should be evolving, exploring their potential, challenging anything of a static nature which could stifle their awareness or impede their progress. A situation in the life of Alfred Duggan serves as a good illustration.

A conscientious and capable man, Alfred gave of his best in his work, and rose successfully in the realms of business administration. On one occasion when faced with a business problem calling for a prompt decision, he found that he could not make up his mind as to what direction he should take. His decision was causing him to be depressed and over-anxious, especially as a strict time-limit increased his sense of urgency and the burden of pressure upon him. Still pre-occupied with the problem and no clear-cut decision in sight, he went to bed, tense but tired.

To his surprise and relief, upon awakening the following morning, he felt refreshed and renewed, with a ready-made solution to the problem in his mind. Tension had left him; and now happy and confident about his decision he resolved on a plan of action.

During the day he discussed strategies with members of his family and a close friend. Each gave a viewpoint as to what action he should take to resolve matters, but all of these views were in conflict, and none agreed with his own independent decision. The effect of this conflicting advice was to undermine his own self-confidence and throw him back into a state of indecision once more. His friend then suggested that he made an appointment to see me, and this was arranged.

During the reading he sat opposite me, rather stiffly and hardly speaking, while listening attentively to what I had to say. I described his position as I saw it, and discussed the action he was likely to take. At the time, I stressed that getting the desired results depended on his keeping to a series of first decisions which, operating in sequence, would provide the scope he needed in the immediate future. Thinking that I had dealt sufficiently with that particular part of the reading, I then focussed my attention on other, but less significant details.

Alfred interrupted me. 'Wait a moment, he said, ' let me tell you something. When I came here today, I wasn't sure what to expect, not having been to anyone like you before. Without asking any questions or knowing anything about me, you have described me as a person, and how I feel, as well as discussing my present problem. Frankly I can't understand how you know these things. You have told me what I should do to solve my business problem, and your solution agrees point for point in every detail with my own personal solution, which came to my mind as I got out of bed three mornings ago. Not only that, you have supplied me with additional details which I had not considered, and which I feel I must think over.'

A question of mind-reading?

He told me about events leading up to his visit to me. One explanation for his earlier silence as I continued with my reading, was that he was astute enough to try to ascertain if I was reading his mind. At that point he did not want to give anything away. I countered that if I had been mind-reading my analysis would be likely to have included one or two 'red herrings' which he would have offered to test me. I reminded him that my profession is that of palmist clairvoyant, not mind-reader.

Alfred Duggan acted in accordance with the course indicated in my reading, and with his own initial decision. I thought afterwards that if he had acted purposefully upon his first impressions of that particular morning when he woke up with a solution in his mind, there would have been no need for him to come and see me subsequently. Apart from his business problem, any other difficulties in his life were well under control for the time being.

I saw that Alfred Duggan was a realist, a methodical thinker, observer and analyst, and the possessor of some considerable driving force. To what extent he was impressed with my hand-reading is not necessarily important; but he clearly valued the usefulness of data obtained through my analysis.

Consider the case of a younger man coming to see me for a consultation. What benefit could he derive from what I could reveal? How, if at all, could this influence his future thinking or prepare him to cope with demanding changes in his way of life - challenges well beyond anything he can imagine at present?

Unsolicited testimonial

What follows is a commentary from one of my clients for whom I made predictions concerning himself, and a certain course of action available to him. His subsequent transition from early self-consciousness to a state of self mastery in which we note the development of his talent and ambition is of interest. I shall call him Russell Farrant. We have observed each other for fourteen years or more; and when in my mind's eye I compare him as he is now with the insecure man he used to be I cannot help but feel elated for him. He has made his own success. The part I have played in it is like that of a silent figure in the background, watching events as they approach and suggesting suitable guidelines as the need arose. However, let him speak for himself.

'I had my first hand-reading with Leonard Flint Ritson fourteen years ago, when I was nineteen. I remember it vividly. I was at a crossroads as far as my career and home life were concerned. Being a reserved person, used to keeping the events of my inner life to myself, I had no-one to talk to at a sufficiently frank and intimate level on these matters. Yet the need to consult a disinterested adult with sensitivity and patience to listen, was strong. Visiting a palmist, whom I did not know, seemed then almost an act of depression; in fact, it was a wise decision.

'The first meeting lasted for about an hour and a half. An immediate rapport was established. Leonard began describing my character. Since we were strangers, the accuracy of this description was in itself startling. I spoke little during the reading, so information about myself could not have been picked up by that means. Having one's character, one's inner life, described in such detail by someone you've never met is a heady experience. It convinced me that I was dealing with a genuine clairvoyant and not someone out to make a fast buck.

My early childhood

'What was more extraordinary was the way he alighted upon early and traumatic events of my childhood which contributed to the shaping of my personality: separation from my mother at birth because she was seriously ill; confusion of the details of what happened to her and the family in those early days; the time spent in a children's home; and later, uncertain and tense relationships within a new family grouping which involved stepsiblings.

'All of these experiences had been bottled up inside me, becoming part of my secret inner world - a secrecy which many adolescents have to preserve if they are to survive in the social groups and institutions they have been assigned to. No-one who thought they knew me at the time could have revealed such central preoccupations in so short a time. It took a clairvoyant to do that.

'Most adolescents are confronted with two fundamental questions: What career shall I follow? When shall I be able to set up my own home? At nineteen, the first question for me was pressing; the second, not being economically possible, had to be reframed as: When can I leave home? I had left school at sixteen (my own decision), taken an apprenticeship in the catering industry, and for a while enjoyed the work. However, it slowly became evident that I was in a career in which I was selling myself short intellectually and socially. The need for a radical change became imperative. But to what? And where? And did I have enough courage to break out of the mould which I had created for myself?

Taking a gamble

'Leonard reassured me that such a change was necessary and imminent; and the decision I would make, which would involve leaving home, would be the right one. I applied to a college of higher education and was accepted at the last minute. Since then, I have made a career in teaching. The social and intellectual stimulation of college life opened up many new channels: I was on my way after a lengthy false start. It is not possible now to pinpoint what gave me the courage to throw up one familiar pattern of existence and take a gamble on another, one which would make far greater demands on me. Undoubtedly, the hand-reading pointed me in the right direction and helped give me an inner certainty that what I was doing was right.

'Since that first meeting I have had several more consultations. They have tended to concentrate on future events, likely outcomes of present arrangements, and as such have been of a predictive nature. I kept notes after each reading of the predictions made, and so the following is based not on the inefficiencies of my memory but on documentary proof.

'It should be said that I got to know Leonard well as a friend, and some of the things said in readings could not help but be influenced by personal knowledge. Sometimes, in fact this personal knowledge may well have hindered rather than helped clairvoyant insight. For instance, at the time I was applying for deputy-headship posts in primary schools I went for a hand-reading, and it was predicted that I would succeed in one of my applications; this, however, failed to come about.

Diary of a client

'Using my notes, I shall now list those events relating to my career which were predicted and have substantially transpired. It should also be said that my notes also indicate a fairly high degree of error in the predictions made, but it would be foolish to expect anything else. It is up to the client to weigh up what has been said, and make what beneficial use of it he can; that is not the palmist's responsibility.

'1974: Two predictions of a similar kind were made. One might have been foreseen by anyone who knew me; the other is a fine example of clairvoyance. A change in job and residential area was predicted for the following year. Even though I had made no plans of this kind, this prediction came about. Much more startling to someone just beginning a teaching career, and rather uncertain of his ability to teach even young children, was a prediction which looked ahead eight years. When you are in your early twenties, anything beyond the age of twenty- five seems light years away.

'Leonard told me that in my thirty-third year, I would move to a more northerly location, would stop teaching children full-time, and would take up a post teaching adults about literature and writing. Four years before I had been just a lowly apprentice doing the most menial jobs in a hotel kitchen. My expectations from life were still low, so wasn't this sort of prediction pie-in-the-sky? I thought so at the time, but duly recorded what had been said in my notes. Now, as I write, I am in just such a job as was described then, a job in a more northerly location which I took up in my thirty-third year!

'1975: A writing project was predicted. It was said that I would write a play in conjunction with someone else, and that the play would be a success. I certainly had no plans for playwriting at the time and, in fact, had never tackled any writing enterprise as substantial as this. I had an ambition to write - a writing career had been repeatedly predicted by Leonard over the years - but for six months I thought no more of this playwriting prospect. Then a friend came to me with a scribbled draft of a three-act play based upon a legend. She asked me if I would 'write it up' as she lacked the necessary skill. I did so, and the play which was enacted by a local dramatic society had a full house for its three-night run. My collaborator acted in the role of leading lady.

1977: 'Leonard predicted that I would write a book in partnership with someone else. Six years later this book looks like coming true. At the time of writing, in collaboration with another adviser, I am putting together a guide to selected children's books, which is being published.

'1979: I was about to move into my first owner-occupied house. Leonard said in a reading that I would be in this house for precisely four years and would make a profit when I came to sell it. Furthermore, when I move I will be living for a time in two houses in different locations, travelling between the two. All these predictions proved to be accurate.

'1982: The job change to adult teaching, predicted eight years ago materialised, and I was in the throes of buying and selling property. I had a reading to help me think this out. Leonard predicted that the purchase deal on the house of my first choice would fall through, and that I would have to accept the second choice. I remember Leonard hesitating when telling me this, as if what he was saying was not quite as clear as it sounded. Subsequent events explained this reticence.

' I made an offer on a house for sale near my new workplace. But the couple buying my existing house withdrew their offer, and the deal fell through, as predicted. I secured a new offer for the house and, on the strength of this, I was able to renew my offer on the house I had originally chosen, and all went well. This is perhaps, an example of clairvoyance pointing the way while not giving the complete picture. Of course, I knew that many house deals fall through, and that what we are talking about here could be coincidence rather than foresight. But in the light of other predictions, one is persuaded to think otherwise.

'My journey from the lowliest of jobs in a hotel kitchen, through college and university, through teaching of young children in several schools, and into teaching of adults at a specialist level, has been helped by the clarification that palmistry can achieve, and by the emotional support it can give at times of doubt - especially self-doubt.

'Other predictions for the future have been made consistently throughout most readings, the two main ones being that I will eventually become a writer; and that I will work abroad a good deal, probably in America and Canada. Only time will show whether these predictiions have, like the others listed above, the force of truth; or whether, like others not mentioned, they fall wide of the mark.

'Whatever happens in the future, I am convinced that the alliance of palmistry and clairvoyance, as practised by Leonard, is capable of producing remarkable results!'

Towards self-knowledge

Russell Farrant continues to make progress towards that desirable state of 'being his own man.' This development has lead to greater insights into what he sees as his own individuality, and his relationship with others, as well as helping in defining his role in life. So far he has gone a considerable way towards knowing himself - an important milestone on the road to emotional maturity.

The future is something tangible to be perceived as a moving, vibrant, creative element extending out of and beyond the present. The future should be seen as being open to change according to the attitudes and impulses which we express. It is usual for human beings to experience ambivalence and dualism in their mental make-up. While being aware of their own achievements, and recognising their limitations, they also cherish secret desires to be elsewhere - to be free to make discoveries and enjoy new experiences.

But man is never as free to make choices as he seems. Where he seeks change which is contrary to the pattern of life pre-ordained in his personal destiny, fate will find a means of manipulating events which take him back towards the course he is meant to follow. Thus his future does not consist only of a series of pre-ordained possibilities which may - or may not - be given the status of reality,according to the individual's response to his circumstances and environment.

CHAPTER 8
Sexual Attitudes

SEXUAL attitudes and patterns of sexual behaviour are indicated by certain line markings and other features on the hand. The nature of a person's sexual drive, his or her response to sexual matters, and any tendency towards deviation, can be identified at one time or another in hand analysis.

Today, a very high percentage of domestic problems are due to inequality of sex factors. It is a fact of life that sex is one of the most powerful forces in human nature. The shape of the hand, the degree of some of the fleshy mounts, as well as the line position upon the palmar surface, contribute towards expressing a person's sexual nature. From these signs we can learn what type of person he is, whether he is erratic and lacks emotional control, whether he has strong sexual tendencies, whether he is an introvert, or bisexual, or sadistic or sexually cold.

When I examine a hand and make an analysis I do not look for one main indication, such as a marriage problem, and straight away begin to describe it. I also look for other influential or contributing factors. Why is there a marriage problem? Which of the partners would be likely to over-react to a stressful situation? How long has the problem been evident? Are children involved and, if so, how will they be affected? What will be the likely outcome? Can the difficulty be overcome and can harmony be restored?

These are the type of questions that pass through my mind as I examine the palm and bring my clairvoyant faculties into play. It is essential that I remain neutral, obviously, and that I speak objectively about what I see, being careful not to express an opinion of my own. More often than not the depth of my concentration leaves me aware only of the hand, wrist and sleeve outstretched before me. Surrounding details, my client's appearance, the decor and furnishing of the room in which we are seated, all remain indistinctly out of focus. I daresay that at such times I would scarcely notice if my client sat in the nude!

For a variety of reasons a woman may continue to tolerate a marital problem which lasts for years; the interests of her children come first; she has no guarantee of financial security were she to leave her husband; divorce may be unacceptable for religious reasons. Or she may love her man sufficiently to stay as she is, and put up with an unhappy situation. In such instances I cannot help but admire her fortitude.

The lines on a person's hand are not fixed to remain in one postion throughout a person's lifetime. They alter in response to changes affecting him and the events of his life. Changes in the lines can also occur over a period in response to intensity of feeling and mental effort.

Dramatic change

Such was the experience of my client, Mary Bartlett. As a prolonged marriage problem altered her outlook on life and her personality, I could see reflected in her hand the prelude to change, the change itself and its aftermath. When I first saw Mary's hand it told me of a subdued nature, of a domesticated woman prepared to play a supporting role in marriage. She appeared to be an incurable romantic who was handicapped by self-consciousness when anything of a practical nature was demanded of her.

The difficulty in her marriage was not of her making. She became a victim. When she understood the nature of her problems, her romantic illusions were replaced by a more practical approach to life. As time passed and as she grew in independence, the need to survive developed in her a dominant quality. In place of her former self- doubt, she became more self-assertive and decisive. She was showing unexpected qualities of leadership and organising ability. At the same time, the sadness and the hollow feeling of betrayal remained always with her.

Mary's story was an interesting one. Her husband, Ron, was a successful self-employed businessman and a good provider. Ron,

Mary and their children lived fairly well; and for years the marriage has every appearance of harmony and stability.

There came a day when, after seeing her husband off to work, Mary decided to turn out the cupboard under the stairs. To her surprise, she came across some ladies' wigs, dresses and underwear which she had never seen before. Troubled at her discovery, her instinct then led her to the shed at the bottom of the garden. Here she found more ladies' clothes, none of which was her own. Although she could hardly bear the thought, she realised this could only point to one thing.

When she confronted Ron about her discovery, he admitted that he was a transvestite. He explained that his performances involved no-one else, that he dressed up in women's clothing only when alone and in private. He dressed up solely for his gratification, and he assured her that he did not belong to any transvestite group or club. He also said that he did not know any other transvestites personally.

Ron had been 'cross-dressing' for a very long time, it transpired. Over the years, he had managed to avoid detection by rising very early and dressing up while the family slept.

Trying to make some sense of her discovery, and recovering somewhat from her initial shock, Mary began to recall unexplained mysteries from the past. There was the time she had come upon a parcel which contained a suspender belt. At the time she assumed that the package was for one of her husband's customers. When once she asked Ron why he got up so early in the morning, he said that he had to keep his business accounts up-to-date. But she found no new entries in the books when she checked up.

Mary immediately drew apart from Ron, but she decided not to let any of the family know about her discovery. For his part, Ron remained silent. Mary moved out of the bedroom she had shared with her husband, insisting that it was now his room alone, and that he was free to do whatever he liked there. She dismissed the thought of legal separation or divorce, because she did not want Ron's practices to become known.

So by mutual consent, Mary and Ron continued to live separate lives within a marriage which had ceased to be a marriage. Little is known of Ron's feelings at this time. He continued as a secret transvestite. Mary felt a deep shame, and even after she had recovered from the main shock, she still had difficulty in accepting what had happened. If her husband had been having an affair with another woman, she could have understood this more readily. But this was something entirely outside her experience.

As far as I know, Mr and Mrs Bartlett are still together. When I last saw them Mary's palms gave no indication that she would have another marriage offer. Nor, indeed, was there any sign of her being interested in such an opportunity.

The variations to be observed in human behaviour clearly are innumerable. Though we are born as individuals, life imposes on us the need to integrate with one another, if only as a self-protective measure. While each one of us is searching for some personal goal, we may never find it. Others are more fortunate in achieving a happy unity between their goal and the reality they come to experience. However much two people may blend together in love and unity, at the same time they must remain individuals. No person can take full responsibility for another; nor is it right to try to do so. We alone are each responsible for ourselves in what we think and do. This is a universal spiritual law, which needs to be better understood.

A state of neutrality

Not all marriage problems due to sexual incompatibility end in divorce, as is generally supposed. A state of neutrality is sometimes reached, whereby husband and wife tacitly agree to compromise and continue to live together, although their differences may cause considerable unhappiness.

The hand of the victim of this sort of marital stalemate often shows indistinct areas of the palm, reflecting doubt and ambivalence in relation to their marriage and family life. Such was the case concerning Elsie Nuttall. Normally an alert, buoyant, sparkling personality, she was listless, subdued and manifestly uneasy in herself when she came to see me.

Her hand revealed the existence of a marriage problem. The first symptom had been a sudden change, which struck at the very foundations of a marriage which had seemed happy and harmonious until then. I told her that she would be parted from her husband, but that I could not see a divorce in store for her. I also said that I thought there was not another woman in her husband's life. Elsie agreed with everything I had said, but contributed nothing further.

Continuing the reading, I referred to her children by the marriage, the question of security in her home-life over the next five years, and detailed her work prospects, which were of considerable importance to her. Her hand showed that her husband would play only a subsidiary role in her life from then onwards; and that the continuing marriage problem was compelling her to adopt a more independent stance. The stumbling block was the clearly-designated neutral zone in her hand. It had been a fate and destiny she could not avoid, thus making her a victim of circumstance. Only by 'living through' this problem could she hope to understand and accept its place in her life, and freely decide on a course of action. So she told me her story.

Elsie had only one real love in her life - her husband Derek. They appeared to be an ideal couple, outwardly living a very happy life with their four children. Derek was loyal, loving and considerate, and there was never any difficulty between them with regard to communication.

By the time all their children were grown-up and beginning to live their own lives, Derek was in his early forties. It was then that the shock came. He left Elsie for a younger *man*! She came for a consultation soon after this event, trying to make sense of what had happened, while attempting to cope with the situation.

Elsie still loved Derek dearly and wanted him back with her. But also she felt too hurt to try to understand his behaviour. For his part, Derek told her that he still loved her, when what he probably meant was that he loved her as a sister. He explained that he must always have had latent homosexual tendencies. His earlier upbringing had been on strict traditional lines. He knew that marriage was expected, and had married partly in order to conform. Sexual education was lacking in his family; in fact, sex was largely a taboo subject at the time.

Forty years on, in the modern age of enlightenment and sexual freedom, where homosexuality had gained acceptance by society, Derek realised his true inclination. Now he was in middle age, the suppressed tendencies of his youth had come to the surface, and he felt he could no longer deny the call of his own nature. He refused to give up his relationship with his new partner, a man younger than his wife.

Elsie still clings to her love for Derek, and he says he still loves her in the way he always has. They live apart, and remain married in name only. Under a new arrangement they meet frequently, but she has not yet learned to accept the other love in her husband's life.

On another occasion, when making an analysis for a professional lady in her early twenties, I observed a striking similarity between the form and markings on her hand to those of Elsie Nuttall's hands.

In this instance, one palm differed in its form from the other. The left hand expressed a sentimental, romantic and home-loving nature, while the right hand showed qualities like energy, ambition, logic, concern for freedom, independence and a vocation for life. The emotional influences seen on the left hand were challenged by the single-minded objectivity shown on the right hand. It made no difference to me, incidentally, whether the young lady was left or right-handed.

My analysis took the usual form of comparing and relating one hand to the other. The left hand shows temperament and potential; indicates how a person began life, and what the future might have been like if he or she had simply waited for opportunities to come along. The right hand relates to change, such as is within the person's capacity. It also shows the possible effect of outside influences, how individuals use free-will to develop their own potential, and in which directions change could take them.

This young lady's sensitivity and background made her a loner, secretly nurturing romantic aspirations which were neither easily expressed nor fulfilled during her early life. In contrast to this tendency she also had a strong instinct for survival, and a practical side to her nature. Moreover, the standards by which she lived would not allow her to accept for long any situation ranking as second best. More than one marriage opportunity was clearly indicated. But the signs were that her best time of life would be in her middle years, which would bring greater happiness and peace than she anticipated at present.

Stale-mate

Julie Warrington lived alone in London and was set to develop a new career in the City. She had a great deal going for her. With good looks, intelligence, an enquiring mind and lively conversational skills, she was a natural organiser. In romantic matters, she appeared to be on the defensive and with additional maturity would be a credit to any man who could win her. She was not an unfriendly type, neither was she openly flirtatious.

The lease on her flat expired before she had time to find another place and an office colleague suggested as a temporary measure that, while searching for somewhere else, she might move into a flat belonging to a male colleague. Julie was glad to take up the offer and it seemed a satisfactory arrangement.

During this period Julie enjoyed the domestic routine and company of her male companion, who was a homosexual and therefore posed no threat. When not working, she found relaxation in the subtle intimacy which developed between them. He was considerate and protective towards her, and interested her in his own cultural and artistic pursuits. Imagine her despair, then, when eventually she realised that she had fallen in love with him; she offered a love which he could not return.

I was faced with the task of describing to Julie the hopelessness of her situation romantically, as shown on her palms. I also tried to help her think of love and marriage on a long-term basis, emphasising the importance of finding another love. I explained that it would not be in her best interests to sever her friendship with the man just then, because it was clear that they enjoyed a harmonious relationship, despite its limitations. Now more than ever she needed warmth, closeness and understanding friendship from a person she valued. A happy marital relationship would come later with another man, I told her.

By its nature my work requires me to be quite close to people with problems. This means that I am in a position to offer sympathy, but this is an urge that I have to resist. Apart from showing a sensitive and sincere reaction when appropriate, I have to insist on maintaining a certain aloofness and detachment, in order to give an objective and constructive analysis.

There are times, as in the case of a prolonged marriage problem, when it would be easy for me to get exasperated at what I see outlined in the hand, and its effect in causing unhappiness for my clients. Through my ability to see ahead to their continuing misery, and realising that they could readily terminate it by divorce, but persist in disregarding the option, I might be tempted to feel impatient. But the one question I never ask is, 'Why do you put up with it?' It is not for me to say what they should or should not do. My own opinion plays no part in my analysis.

No matter how familiar a client is with his problem, he is likely to have missed out in considering perspectives and the possible solutions which are offered through analysis. The explanation is that when you are very closely involved in the circumstances of the situation, it is virtually impossible to take an overall view. By studying the different approaches to the problem, and helping the client to stand aside, as it were, and look at the whole picture - not just a small part of it - it is often possible to change the client's outlook entirely, so that there is a resurgence of hope and self-confidence. Seeing such a rediscovery of hope and identity makes this aspect of my work very rewarding.

Minority taste

I recall the case of a woman who had been coming to see me for a number of years. At an early stage, I had predicted a marriage break for her - long before it happened. I had warned her repeatedly that this would happen, as her hand showed this pattern of events very clearly. One can attempt to prevent such a crisis by giving warning and allowing time for matters to improve. However, in this woman's case, conditions in the marriage deteriorated further, as time went by.

She was an ordinary woman with a normal sex-drive. She wanted above all to be loved and cherished in a secure permanent relationship. Yet her warm and affectionate nature was stifled by her husband's continuing coldness, for which she could find no explanation. On the rare occasions he made love to her, he performed his part mechanically, dispassionately and quickly, without any show of affection at any stage. Feeling neither fulfilled nor satisfied with the relationship, she was too sincere and loyal to consider having a lover.

In studying her hand I saw a crisis approaching. I stressed the necessity of divorcing her husband, but told her that I could not see any other woman in her husband's life. She stubbornly refused to consider the idea of divorce and went her way. Within a short time the storm broke. Unexpectedly, she came to see me, white-faced, distressed, indignant. The prelude to her anguisehed story was a frenzy of name-calling against her husband, as the pent-up frustration of years found expression and release. And she was ready to start divorce proceedings.

Her husband, Johnnie, was a skilled manual worker who

earned extra money by using his skills in his own workshop. Countdown to the dramatic climax in their marriage began when his wife was turning over the mattress of his bed one morning. Underneath, she discovered a number of very explicit 'hard porn' magazines which featured sexual perversions, bondage, flagellation, bestial behaviour, and group sex practices - a veritable sexual circus.

She kept the magazines as evidence, and bided her time while keeping a watch on her husband's behaviour. About this time she decided in her own mind that divorce really was the only solution to her problems.

Not long afterwards, she went out one evening to attend a meeting, telling her husband she would be back at the usual time . When she got to the hall she found the meeting had been cancelled at short notice. Returning home early, she was horrified to find her husband indulging in one of the sexual perversions shown in one of the magazines. Her story has a happy ending, however, for in due course she obtained a divorce, and eventually remarried.

Procreaction is an important function of the human race which has social and religious implications. Obviously the selection of a mate is of vital significance in this process; I am convinced that in the majority of cases it is the women that choose their men. A man may desire a woman, succeed in having an affair with her, even persuade her to marry him. His success can work wonders for his ego and self-image, but he is unlikely to admit that he succeeded in his quest because the lady permitted him to do so.

The same man could meet a woman, desire her, get to know her a little, and propose marriage in the belief that he is the answer to her prayer (and she to his). But if she is not interested in his proposal, there is not much he can do to get her to change her mind in his favour. An exceptional case is that of the woman caught on the rebound after a disappointment in love. Then she might allow herself to be more perceptive to the attentions of a newcomer, because he offered her security and status in marriage. Later, she might choose a different man altogether to satisfy her romantically. Man is not always the hunter.

CHAPTER 9
Missed Opportunities

THE dominion of the unknown and unseen holds within its grasp the key to the purpose of existence. Man's capacity to explore the range of his consciousness and intelligence has increased enormously in the twentieth century. The resultant broadening of his outlook has made him more aware of the occult sciences of which palmistry is a part.

The realisation that the power of mind is not bounded by time and space has led to the rediscovery of ancient sciences. And so we find that within the evolutionary cycle nothing is really new because it has already existed in some form in an earlier epoch.

Just as it is possible to predict the future and move forward in time, the same law makes it possible to go backward in time. 'As it was in the beginning, is now, and ever shall be,' is a statement of religious principle, which also expresses a truth of occult significance.

I do not believe in thrusting the merits of palmistry at anyone. I prefer them to discover for themselves that it can be of tremendous value in increasing self-knowledge and problem-solving. Knowing its potential, I never worry about those who dismiss palmistry as hocus-pocus. There is always something new to learn about palmistry and people. No matter how familiar I am with a situation or a person's category, however much my intuition tells me that my assessments or predictions are correct, I know I still have to consider the doubter who cannot believe that there is even an element of truth in palmistry.

Having blocked off an important part of their nature, doubters choose not to develop their awareness, and so lose out on the choices offered to them at certain stages in life, sometimes to their cost. They learn the realities of life the hard way. I do not allow such attitudes to affect me personally, because all I have to do is to tell a client what I see. In my role as palmist, I am the receiver and transmitter of information for the client. And if someone decides not to act upon the guidance given there is nothing I can do about it.

Reliving a nightmare

About eleven years ago, a man whose identity I never knew paid me a visit. A man of brisk mind and taut dispostion, he had been born with an excess of nervous energy. I had completed my reading and he was preparing to leave when he turned to me. 'Well, you haven't told me anything of my past,' he said.

'I did not think that was relevant,' I replied. 'I thought it more important to you that I concentrated on the present and future.'

'But you still have not told me anything of my past,' he persisted, with an aggressive edge to his voice.

I took hold of his hand - he had ugly thumbs - and concentrated for some moments. Then I gave my answer, with Cis - we were now in the sitting room - present as witness.

I described an incident in which he had been involved some years earlier. I saw him engaged in an argument with a young woman who might be his girl-friend. The dispute became more heated and he lost control of himself. In a rage, he grasped the woman around the throat with both hands, and began to squeeze. No matter how she struggled to free herself, she could not loosen his grip. Her body began to go limp although she was still standing.

Coming to his senses and realising the enormity of his action, the man released the woman and made attempts to revive her. In a short time she seemed to have recovered. The scene ended, or at least that was all I saw of it.

He stood in front of me, his face drawn and mask-like, and drained of colour. No words were exchanged between us, and he made for the door. Once outside he seemed undecided as to which way he wanted to go. He muttered something about needing a drink. Then, turning to face the open doorway he looked straight at me and said, 'I do not like anyone knowing that much about me, least of all a stranger.' I stared straight back at him, saying nothing. He dropped his gaze, turned on his heel and walked away into the night, never to return.

In my examination of this man's hand the incident I described to him was the first impression which came into my mind's eye as a complete picture. It was a shock disclosure as to a part of his nature which he would prefer to conceal. He was not content with the information I had given him earlier in the reading. He wanted more, and got it.

I do not have to interpret the meaning of everything I see in a client's hand. But neither must I deviate from the truth in my description of factors which provide the impression on which I base my interpretation. If I slow down my thinking pace to over-analyse whatever I see, then there is a risk that I may allow my personal logic to come into play and distort basic impressions. I keep an open mind for every reading; but, as much as any of my clients, I need proof that my predictions are correct. And, as I have already shown, events forecast in advance very often come to pass, as my clients come back to testify themselves.

An expensive mistake

Alistair McPhee was a likeable man, with a strong personality and a warm nature, who enjoyed the good things of life. His ready wit and lively repartee made him excellent company on any social occasion. He had travelled and seen something of the world and there was a certain charm in his devotion to life and its enjoyments.

Alistair was a canny Scot and something of a sceptic, with the shrewdness of mind deriving from business experience. I liked him at once. In my first analysis for him I described in detail an impending divorce and its accompanying emotional trauma. I perceived that he was by nature one of those who prefer a direct approach when being given painful tidings, and that this was the only way to hold his attention, respect and trust. My reading mirrored his own thoughts and actions up to that moment. Quietly and dispassionately, I told him of the strengths and weaknesses in his strategy to reshape his domestic and business life.

His hands were nicely shaped and in good proportion, and strong and expressive in their features. Apart from the matter of his forthcoming divorce, I foresaw a seemingly lucrative business proposition being offered to Alistair by a colleague already known to him. On his right hand I saw an accompanying sign relating to this business venture which indicated that the scheme carried a considerable risk of failure - something which his left hand had not suggested clearly.

If both hands carry the same mark in identical places on the palm, it is reasonable if not safe to conclude that what is shown there will happen. This applies whether a situation is influenced by external events over which the subject has only limited control, or whether it involves the exercise of his own initiative and free-will.

I was not satisfied that if offered a business opportunity of this kind Alistair would necessarily understand what he was taking upon himself. I described to him in detail the proposed arrangement, how it would be implemented, and what it involved. I followed this up by counselling him that he should not take up the proposition for several reasons. These included the high cost of his stake in the venture; the fact that more than one person featured in the capacity of 'business partner', and ambiguity about the question of business policy. If Alistair disagreed with his partners on some technicality, for instance, then he could be out-voted and obliged to follow a policy of which he did not approve. I was concerned that he would lose money in the venture, and told him so. The time was not right for him to consider a business partnership.

During the same reading, I went on to reassure Alistair that he should not be too disappointed at losing a business opportunity because I could see that a much sounder offer would come his way within a matter of months, one which would involve work of an altogether different kind. I was able to round off the reading by predicting the development of a new romantic relationship in his life. This clearly pleased him, as he was quite a virile man with a strong sex-drive and at the moment he was ready for a stimulating adventure.

Alistair came to see me again several months later and I could see he was in trouble. He was very agitated and entirely different in manner and appearance from the self-assured man I had seen at our first meeting.

Despite my warning he had accepted a business partnership

with two colleagues and had invested most of his collateral security in the enterprise. Almost immediately the venture began to backfire. The money invested in the scheme was not enough and more had to be raised to support it. Alistair could not afford the price of his commitment but, feeling that he could not back down now, found himself getting deeper into debt. The business continued to lose money, until it was eventually put into the hands of the official receiver.

Cis, my lady companion, witnessed my second consultation with Alistair. Listening to his tale of woe, and his references to our earlier meeting, she asked him why he had chosen to disregard my warning about the business offer. He said that he had been extra careful following the original consultation. He had checked and rechecked all the details relating to the project, and concluded that he had a better first-hand knowledge of the practical side of the business than I realised. In other words, he thought that his own assessment of the situation was accurate, and that mine was wide of the mark.

'It was an expensive mistake, though, all the same, wasn't it, Alistair?' Cis said, and he had to agree. However, I am pleased to say that there were happier times ahead for him. When I had known him for about three years he moved away to another part of the country. As I predicted, a second business opportunity materialised, which he accepted, though it meant moving again. Somehow or other he had managed to raise the capital required, sell his house, complete his divorce proceedings and start life afresh. Although it took all the money he could raise, I understand the venture is a success, and his courage in rising to this new challenge has paid dividends.

Three valuable years

I also suspect that there is a new love in Alistair's life, and I wish them well, but I cannot help reflecting occasionally on the serious set-backs he could so easily have avoided. Solving the resultant problems and re-establishing himself financially took at least three valuable years out of his life, which could have been put to better and happier use had he acted more wisely.

When I meet clients for the first time, I consider it useful for me to give a brief analysis of their character and personality at the beginning of the reading. As a stranger, giving them information about themselves - sometimes which only they know - my aim is to help the client to get used to me and to the technique I use in my work. Having, as I hope, put them at their ease, I then move my analysis forward to describe what is happening at that particular time in their lives, and what their future portends.

However, when clients come to see me a number of times I try to dismiss what I already know about them. I do this to minimise any influence the client may have on me, either intentionally or otherwise. By then they should have a better understanding of my method of making an analysis. For myself, I find it necessary to start with my mind blank; the client settles into the chair opposite me, and I begin examining each palm in turn.

At this point, the process starts operating and I begin receiving impressions. As I explained earlier, I see the palm as a map and further details are obtained clairvoyantly. The question may arise as to what I should do if clients continually disregard my counselling on the subject of their career and business prospects. The answer is that I cannot interfere. The client must be left free to decide. But I must admit that it can be very frustrating to have to stand helplessly by, knowing that a client would be risking disaster by ignoring my assessment.

The best-laid plans

A case in point was that of a married couple who came together to see me about their future business prospects. They had recently opened a boutique. Both had strong personalities, but the wife appeared to be the dominant partner. More often than not, it was her decisions which prevailed. The impression I got from an examination of both their hands was that neither was suited for the work such a shop demanded, that they were the wrong type of people to be running such a business.

The boutique was in a lovely setting and its decor could not be faulted. A great deal of thought had gone into planning the interior design in a very tasteful style, combining elegance and comfort. Needless to say it had taken considerable expense to achieve this result.

I was convinced, however, that my first impression was the correct one. The business would not succeed for a number of reasons. The location was wrong for this type of venture, which would have fitted perfectly into to a city setting, but not in an out-of-the-way town with a small and somewhat elderly population. From the start the boutique had failed to attract the custom of local people.

Both pairs of hands showed the principal lines of their palms to be similar, emphasising the situation which they shared and experienced. The wife's hand showed a more determined nature capable of reacting strongly against opposition to her own wishes. The identical area of the husband's hand showed similar line markings, except that in his case the lines were decidedly thicker or broader in appearance. This confirmed a greater sense of caution on his part. He was a man swept along by circumstances rather than by his own decision to challenge or control the condition in which he found himself. Without his wife's influence, indicated by the marriage mark upon his palm, he would by his own natural and free choice have aimed for an altogether different kind of role than that of a boutique owner . Obviously the course of his life would have been very different.

The advantage at times of having two people together for a hand- reading is that the chirologist can see the attitudes expressed on both sides simultaneously. He is thus able to assess the nature of the common denominator linking both partners, such as a shared driving force. Consequently if one person is ahead of the other in terms of ability, will-power, perception or ambition, then the palmist can judge whether or not an aim subscribed to by only one member could have a lasting influence on the other. He can also judge whether the dominant partner's leadership is ever likely to be challenged, and to what extent the couple are compatible.

It was these parallel courses shown in the hands of this couple which interested me most. It seemed to me to resemble a tortoise and hare situation, with the husband being the slower and more cautious of the two. But in his quiet reserve lay hidden strength and I foresaw the possibility of a change of role between them in the future.

The man himself had a certain dignity of bearing and an expressive though careworn face. His eyes were set a trifle deep so that it was not always easy to see their expression, but when they moved the whites caught the light and flashed with unexpected intensity. The modelling of his features was similar to the style often depicted by El Greco, or so I thought. And fortune had endowed him with enough talent to make a mark in the artistic world. At least he preferred the artist's canvas to the world of fashion, and hence this was the cause of some of the degree of the conflict which registered within himself.

For her part, the wife looked for a different kind of understanding from people to that which she usually experienced. The pressure to which she subjected herself in the day-to-day running of the business needed to be counter-balanced by closer emotional interchanges within marriage than were usually available. Though the last thing she wanted to be was a solitary person, she was often tempted to retreat into a world of her own.

Over a four-year period I watched their business hopes rise and fall, with no sign of a worthwhile profit materialising. The boutique continued in business, and thousands of pounds were spent in vain attempts to make it successful. Repeatedly, until I imagined I sounded rather like a phonograph recording, I told them both, 'Call it a day. You have both tried so hard, and it is not a disgrace for you to fail. Destiny is acting against you, and it must be for a reason. Take heed of it. Spend no more. Shut the door. Cease business.'

The last consultation I gave them was an embarrassing one. Neither spoke as they each waited to hear my predictions. Carefully I re-examined their hands. To me, it was like going over old ground, because there was nothing new to tell them.

'There is nothing fresh to add to what I told you before,' I told them. 'I cannot alter my prediction that, unfortunately, the business cannot succeed. Finish it now and close the door.'

They both looked sad and dejected. His eyes were dull, lacking any suggestion of sparkle. He looked a tired man. She stared straight at me and said, 'I know. You have been right all along.' Tears spilt from the corners of her eyes, as she looked down at her lap to conceal them from me. Recognition of the truth had come too late for them. Soon the boutique closed and the building changed from business premises to a domestic dwelling.

Privately, my thoughts were that if the couple had accepted my earliest prediction some years previously, they could have avoided this heartbreak and achieved a considerable saving of capital. I indulged myself in the notion that had they given me ten per cent of the money which they had lost over the past two years, I could have invested it and returned half to them in their time of need.

I could see that the years ahead would be difficult for the

couple,yet despite the setbacks the marriage would hold together. With the support of his close family and relations, he planned to change his life, so that earning a living depended more on the development of his artistic talents.

I find that a proportion of those who come to me for guidance arrive with a preconceived idea of what it is they want to hear. However, my analysis may differ from this considerably, and I cannot alter what I see in my assessment. Sometimes on such occasions I get the impression that the client is not really listening to what I have to say, but for my part I will still not alter what I see, to suit their purposes.

I am reminded here of a visit paid to me by Cyril Ambrose, a conscientious, hard-working man I had known socially for some years. He knew of my work and did not criticise or condemn it when it featured in conversation, but kept an open mind about it. He was prepared to go a considerable way towards believing in the function and usefulness of my work; but he was nevertheless the sort of man who needed additional proof of its validity.

Family business

Cyril's visit was a pleasant surprise, and I was about to settle for an informal chat when, out of the blue, he asked me to give him a reading. This was to be his second analysis from me, as I had read his hands once before, some years previously. He did not object to a relative being present during the reading. His hands were strong, square, of the practical type and well shaped, with a hint of good breeding in the family line. His fingernails were of good shape and texture, and his skin was clear and healthy.

Mentally I dissociated myself from him as a person, and made a conscious effort to dismiss from my mind everything I already knew about him until, clairvoyantly, I was looking at a blank screen. I remained silent, waiting, while I gathered together my impressions and observations. My silence was not intended to have an effect upon my audience; if anything, this pause was necessary to help me make my assessment.

The reading included interesting details. I was able to describe matters of a speculative nature, commercial finance and business structure. Cyril seemed to be listening intently, but did not comment.

I learnt afterwards from the relative who had been present that she thought my reading had taken the wrong approach entirely. My reference to stocks and shares and other financial matters seemed particularly inappropriate. Cyril's life had not been an easy one up to the stage of near retirement. Born of a good family, he had sought independence as a young man still in his teens, and he had married early in life.

A sensitive survivor, he shared with many others of his time the rigours and uncertainty of the 1930's Depression in Britain; and perhaps this experience left him with an element of scepticism in his make-up. A man of courage and conviction, he made it clear to others that he was a law unto himself. He could be depended upon to stand his ground in defence of a cause close to his heart. His progress in life was due to his own initiative and hard work. He asked for few favours, and accepted no hand-outs from people he knew. His cautious nature led him to plan carefully each step in his pursuit of security, being careful to avoid risks of any sort. He was not a gambler.

Yet here was I, confronting this self-sufficient man with details of an opportunity to invest capital safely and profitably. I told Cyril that he would be approached by those negotiating the deal, and that it would turn out to be a wise investment, yielding a high dividend. But he would have to make up his mind quickly.

Feeling that I had exhausted this subject, I went on to discuss aspects of the more distant future. I began to describe a possible family problem which would involve him in some way. I did not get any further because at that point Cyril interrupted me, saying, 'That's fine, you have gone far enough.' He paused, his hands now free from my inspection, and shifted his position. Putting his hand into his jacket pocket he took out a sheet of green paper.

'What you have said is very interesting,' he said. 'I have with me a document which I received at work this morning, offering me the chance to buy some shares in the private company that I work for, before it goes public. No-one other than my associates has seen it; not even my wife knows about it yet. This is the reason for my visit to you today. I wanted to see if you could detect this ocurrence, and if you could tell whether the offer is a sound one. I was hoping you could advise me as to what I should do about it.'

As is common with my readings, I rarely ask my client any questions, preferring instead to give them the information which comes to me through a combination of palmistry and clairvoyance.

The outcome of his reading was two-fold. Cyril took advantage of the business shares offer and his investment repaid him with a gain of 100 per cent. The woman relative who attended the reading also benefited, as Cyril was able to buy her a number of shares at the same time.

The second prediction took longer to materialise. It related to my reference to a family matter, at which point Cyril cut me short. In the period following his profitable speculation, a serious family problem did arise, which placed him in an awkward situation and required him to come to the assistance of certain members of his family. The aid which he gave to his family made it necessary among other things for him to spend approximately the equivalent amount of capital that he had made from the business shares. Speculation on one side, a family problem on the other; the final issue was one where Cyril's finances broke even.

Had he not prevented me from concluding the reading, he might have been wiser before the event. And with fore-knowledge, he might even have been able to help forestall the family crisis which cost him so dearly. At the least it did some good, if not altogether for Cyril himself, then for others, and so an allegiance to conventional standards of conduct, that which is right, was upheld.

CHAPTER 10
Matters of Life and Death

I HAVE never been one to dwell too long on the subject of death. At one stage in my youth I thought that when my own time came, all that mattered, provided I died with dignity and bravely if sacrifice was called for, was that I would conduct myself in the manner of Sydney Carton meeting La Guillotine in Dickens' 'A Tale of Two Cities'. 'It is a far, far better rest that I go to than I have ever known.' I did not really see myself as an heroic figure, though the idea of a dignified exit had its appeal.

A long time ago I remember hearing some people talking about the tragic sinking of the Titanic. As each member of the group speculated about the last hours of doomed passengers on the stricken liner, whose sad fate was to drown, I was brought into the conversation, and placed like a collage in the scene. Someone said, 'Ah yes, Leonard would give up his position in a lifeboat for a woman or child; he would remain calm and without trace of panic.'

In those days I was rather formal in manner, brought up to think that outward appearances must be maintained at all costs, it was unpardonable folly to disclose any inner feelings whether they contained depth or not. I asked myself then (and repeat the question now), whether I would feel fear in such a situation. I am sure that I would, but I am now convinced that there is nothing shameful about being fearful in a very frightening situation. Fear is one of the barriers we all must learn to overcome, as we face life and death in the fullness of time.

I do not go out of my way to look for death signs when making an analysis for clients. My life has been such that I did not see a corpse at first hand until I was over 22 years of age. I was too young to be aware of events at Auschwitz, Ravensbruck and Buchanwald, except by means of authentic film coverage much later. My only involvement in a war situation was when I was a baby and much too young to understand what was going on; for all of which I am grateful, so there would be no real cause for me to preoccupy myself with death to any great extent.

My spiritual faith and awareness convinces me that if all there was to human life was three score years and ten, then how futile all our efforts would be. Even if we accepted this theory, it would still leave many vital questions unanswered. What is the source of wisdom, for example? Wisdom is not achieved by education but is an inborn quality possessed by an individual. Certain wisdom is also imbibed in those who have not lived long enough to gain wisdom from experience alone. Nevertheless, such a gift of wisdom is for me evidence of pre-existence. According to the same natural law there is no end to end itself, but rather a new beginning.

Those who disagree with me on this point must follow their own concepts and inner convictions. My own beliefs are important to me, and would still be if no-one else shared them. The beauty and wisdom of the 23rd Psalm of David in the Old Testament is in itself the key towards 'that which passes all understanding'. As a youngster, hearing a famous hymn during school assembly, I would think that to be a pilgrim seemed a fine vocation, provided one did not become a 'grim pill', and by too serious an outlook cloud the pleasures that life offers. It should be left to everyone to decide for themselves at what level they wish to develop their minds and souls through esoteric knowledge.

Links with the past

It is wonderful that a spiritualist medium can establish a link with those who have gone before us and, furthermore, can make contact with Uncle Willie who died in action in the Great War, or that a link is made with Eleanor who once lived in Kensington and who had a parrot. This phenomenon must in its information be of value and comfort to the bereaved people who miss Uncle Willie or Eleanor.

I am more interested in the source from which such knowledge may be obtained. I feel that the capacity to tune in spiritually can be of tremendous importance for us all, but in particular to students of the occult who desire to learn more of its scope and impact. This is the essential difference between a spiritualist and an occultist.

To obtain enlightenment and put it to correct use a simple law must be observed. This is that a balance must be maintained. Examples of balance are evident in the correlation between ying and yang. To appreciate the workings of good, the right-hand path in esotericism, it is necessary to understand evil and its ways, that which is of the left-hand path. Another example of balance is evident in the polarity of the earth and the polarity of the electromagnetism of human beings.

Where the balance is not sustained, the desired result cannot be achieved and distortion or extremes act in its place. Occasionally among the many types of clients' problems I encounter I have to try to help someone with suicidal tendencies. The inclination to self-murder can be seen in the lines shown on the hand. The shape of the hand sometimes provides an additional clue, and the combination of certain details including a 'death sign' (known as such in palmistry) can be the conclusive pointer confronting the chirologist.

When I began practising as a palmist, I had to decide for myself whether or not I could face the more serious problems likely to be met in the course of this work. I decided in favour of a direct and open policy, on the basis that every problem is a natural part of life itself. No matter how delicate - or serious - the problem perceived, there was little or nothing that could not be discussed, provided that the client was approached in the right way. If I lacked the courage to face serious issues even as an observer, digressed to dwell on irrelevancies or side-issues without giving crucial guidance to my client, then I would not feel that I was doing my work properly or efficiently.

In all, I met Sandra Mitchell four times; twice with her mother, once on her own, and once in the company of her boy-friend. On the first occasion, I detected evidence in her hands of confused aims in her life, conflict with her family, a need within herself to be alone, and an inevitable drift towards disillusionment and suicide. I decided then and there to give her a straightforward assessment of her nature and capacity for self-destruction. Looking at her, I was surprised to find such an inner sense of defeat at work behind such a self-assured and attractive personality, and I reminded myself not to be swayed by appearances.

At that meeting Sandra wished her mother to stay with her during the consultation. Knowing what to say, yet weighing the words in my mind to see how best to phrase what needed to be said, I glanced casually in her mother's direction. There was not overmuch resemblance between the two, suggesting that Sandra probably took after her father with regard to looks. Her hand told me that there was a spasmodic affinity between mother and daughter, and a lesser degree of closeness between Sandra and her father. Proceeding, I decided to ignore the mother's presence, and concentrated on my assessment.

I described to Sandra what I saw of her complex nature, which meant that she could enjoy life fully one minute and then plummet irrationally to the depths of despair. There were times when she disregarded everyone and everything around her. She experienced moods during which she was aimless and indifferent; there were times when she did not care that she did not care. I explained how during these latter phases she could reach a dangerous pitch, wish herself dead and be actually capable of taking her own life.

Shock tactics

As I spoke to her, I looked directly at her, making eye-to-eye contact. By not mincing words I hoped to shock her, because I did not think a gentle, soothing approach would have any effect. I wanted to jolt her off her course towards self-murder. There was silence between us then. Her face lost its colour, reflecting instant panic and a desire to run away and hide. Then her tears came, openly and unrestricted, releasing some of her inner tension, as I held her right hand in mine and pressed it reassuringly.

'You do understand the depths to which you can sink, do you not?' I asked her.

'Yes,' she replied.

'You do understand that you have the capacity to take your life, and that it would not be a theatrical gesture on your part, where you would intend to be found in time to be saved? The suicidal urge you are capable of expressing would be the real thing, a finish for you, don't you see?'

After a pause she answered more firmly this time, 'Yes.'

'Then snap out of it,' I exhorted. 'Get it into your head for once in your life that you are of worth to others and to yourself. Stop being so negative about everything.' Her mother had not uttered one word. For a moment we both sat quietly watching her daughter.

'Enough of the agony, Sandra,' I said eventually. 'I would like to continue and tell you of more hopeful signs I see in the life ahead.'

At that time Sandra had no romantic interest in her life. She found it easy to talk and seemed to appreciate my direct approach, and the fact that I was a total stranger. I told her how in time ahead she would be wooed and courted, and she smiled shyly, showing her pleasure.

Sandra had a beautiful smile, and the type of features which were nearly classical. In my mind's eye I could see a silhouette of her features as adorning some ancient Grecian villa, or being used as the inspiration for a Wedgwood vase. Beyond her pain one could detect glimpses of colour and warmth and gaiety, which augered well for the future, despite her current problems.

I was correct in my prediction about her romantic prospects. She came back one day, bringing with her a steady, upright young man whose interests and work were concerned with nature and conservation. She was the happiest I had ever known her to be. Nervous of marriage, but with enough trust in the relationship to live with her lover, she was happy to have obtained her parents' blessing.

Her young man clearly loved her. He was strong and capable, and there was nothing he would not do for her. She appeared to lean on him. But I was dismayed when I analysed her hand, because I saw a dark cloud on the horizon which I could not dismiss. I detected a return of her earlier stresses which I had hoped were a thing of the past. I could not but feel worried for her. She knew that I knew about these feelings. So I merely touched on the problem lightly by saying, 'Be happy for now, Sandra. Take one day at a time, and don't slip backwards.' To her young man, who shared the consulation, I said 'Look after her, and see that she does as she is told.' At which we all laughed.

Some days later, I received through the post a package containing a small, finely-bound book of poems. As it happened it was a book I had been seeking for a long time. Written inside it was a message of thanks for the hope and uplift that Sandra said I had given her.

The cloud I had seen had not moved away.

After some months her mother visited me. I learnt that Sandra had broken off the relationship with the young man I had met and gone to live for a time in a cottage provided by her parents. Then one day, carefully and deliberately, Sandra took her own life in a situation where it was not possible to save her. She died young, and in the background of everything that occurred around her lay an illness of which I know little. Sandra had developed and suffered from the slimmers' disease, anorexia nervosa, and her beauty, which others saw, for her did not exist.

There are some people who cannot live by themselves, let alone cope well with any solitary period in their lives. These are the type of people who dread Sundays, when the fast, overbearing pace of the week gives way to a quiet tempo. Few public places are open and most people are satisfied to limit their activities temporarily to the home circle. The ones who find quietness and stillness alarming tend to be those who need to be at the centre of constant noise and activity, in order to feel that their lives are justified.

Social outcast

Loneliness is a blight on society , a malady which affects a large percentage of the population. Divorced people are often lonely and their friends and relations are not always aware of their plight. The young divorced woman often becomes something of a social outcast. Her married women friends may view her as a threat to the security of their own marriages. It is all too easy for her to become the odd one out, who is difficult to include in their social plans.

Judy Richardson was in this position. The humiliation of her divorce brought about by her husband's misconduct and disloyalty was a blow from which she never recovered. As the mood is reflected in the hand, the tell-tale signs of despair were well established when I first made an analysis of her palms.

She developed a drinking problem, which rapidly became more acute. Her two grown-up children lived their own lives; one was in London and the other was abroad. The lighter side of Judy's once fun-loving nature was rarely seen these days. When we met I did my best to give her buoyancy. But this was hard going, and her moody, oppressive nature became deadweight.

Her symptoms were pointing in one direction, downwards

towards suicide. I warned her of this risk many times and tried by various means to make her realise her state and come to her senses. The humorous approach, the sincere yet serious approach, shock tactics, all my methods towards her had limited effect; the inevitable drew closer. The situation was extremely frustrating, and my own position was rather like that of Canute trying to hold back the incoming tide.

My telephone would ring at midnight. It would be Judy, the worse for drink, an odd wailing moan sounding in her voice as she sought sympathy and guidance which she was unlikely to follow. There would be a momentary uplift, gratitude for reassurance, hope fighting against lack of confidence, and then emptiness, the recurring crash, solace in a bottle, a predictable cycle time and time again. Midnight, my telephone would ring; it would be Judy.

A time came when I spent a few days away from home. During the week following my return I read a newspaper report of Judy's fatal drug overdose. Christmas was not far off. I think that she desperately wanted a family reunion, and particularly at this time of the year, but sadly this did not seem possible. Perhaps she tried to telephone me, and I wasn't there, and only silence and emptiness remained, a tragic legacy for her.

Back from the brink

By contrast, it is uplifting to see someone who was once clearly suicidal returned to a sense of purpose, harmony and love, having left behind once and for all a stark period of despair and desolation in which the edge of the abyss was perilously close. Such is the story of Margaret Foster.

For her, the downward spiral began slowly, almost imperceptibly. At first glance there was nothing to suggest any serious adversity in her life-style, which appeared outwardly calm, ordinary and conventional. Margaret was an only child. Both her parents were dead and she had no surviving relatives. She had inherited her parents' estate and now she was married with a young baby and a husband whom she loved dearly, and trusted absolutely. Consequently, she willingly put her inheritance into a joint bank account. Her husband undertook to pay bills as they arose, as well as making mortgage payments on the house they were buying.

Margaret's hands showed her to be of a nervous disposition, not very practical, not at all career minded and more suited to playing a supporting role. Domesticated and incurably romantic, she combined a possessive nature with warmth, humour and naivety.

Two marriages were palmistically indicated for her. When I examined the relevant area of Margaret's palms more closely, I construed that a second marriage opportunity would arise for her, not out of an illicit amour but more due to the breakdown of her present marriage. Considerable stress was shown to lie ahead in the practical and financial spheres of her life; and she would suffer the effects of over-reaction to the termination of her marriage.

I consider it important when making a hand analysis not to keep the client waiting too long to hear my observations. It usually takes nearly a minute of silent study before I speak. A longer interval might cause the client to feel unnecessarily tense and apprehensive, and with his or her mind thus preoccupied, it may be difficult to take in what the palmist has to say.

Therefore in the early moments of a hand-reading my mind is required to work very rapidly. Rather in the manner of a computer, it has to assimilate details revealed, and arrange them in some form of order (in terms of importance or chronological sequence) which will be understandable to the client.

When evidence of a marriage problem is visible on a client's hand, I believe in a straightforward approach to the matter, while maintaining for myself a neutral stance. It can be said that some women are emotionally orientated, compared with men who tend in the main to be motivated by practical considerations, finding a down-to-earth approach of much greater tactical value in everyday life. At no time would I deliberately set out to break a marriage; rather the reverse. If more than one marriage is indicated on a person's hand, the reason must be examined and if possible explained, and thereafter the individual's free-will has a role in deciding the outcome.

I stressed to Margaret the importance she placed on feeling loved and appreciated. I then began to describe what I had seen in her palms, expressing my fears about incompatibility between herself and her husband. I advised her to observe the situation and not to panic. Where possible she should do all she could to strengthen her marriage, although in fact up to that time she had considered her marriage safe and secure. She did not fully agree with everything I said, possibly because she did not want to face the full impact of my analysis, but she nevertheless promised she would do what she could towards improving her marriage.

At her third visit to me, it was clear that problems had intensified, and marriage difficulties had arisen. Her husband had walked out on her, leaving her alone in their house with her baby son. Bewildered and unhappy, Margaret could form no clear plan of action in her mind. She asked my advice. I analysed the situation, telling her that, from my reading of her hand, there did not seem to be another woman in her husband's life at that time, and that he would want to come back to her. I warned her of future instability in the marriage in the event of a reconciliation and observed in that event she was likely to have a second child.

I could see an ambivalence in Margaret's attitude to her problems. On the one hand she was developing a practical, defensive side of her nature. On the other, she was preoccupied with the romantic aspects of her marital relationship which, inevitably, left her open to further let-down in the future.

Her husband did return some time later and, as I predicted, she conceived and had her second child, a girl. While she was in hospital for the birth, he visited her and saw the new baby. But, just before she was due to go home, he left her for a second time, taking their car with him.

Nor did he go alone. On this occasion he was accompanied by the wife of a neighbour who lived in the same street. The couple had been married for barely a year, and they had no children. Margaret's husband was not seen in the area again. It then came to light that over the years he had squandered all the money in their joint bank account. He had not paid the household bills for a considerable period, nor had he kept up the mortgage payments on the house. Furthermore, he left other debts. It was also revealed that he was a heroin addict, possibly spending a colossal sum every day to maintain the habit.

In great distress, Margaret telephoned asking if I could possibly visit her, which I did. Her torment was so extreme that she clearly was in a suicidal state. I encouraged her to pour out her troubles while I listened quietly, as I felt it was important that she should not feel alone at a time like this; having someone to talk to would help to release some of the tension. She told me that she felt like taking her own life, and repeated this a number of times in the course of her monologue.

Everything to live for

I tried to calm her and then openly pleaded with her not to do anything to endanger her life. I stressed the need to survive for the sake of her children, pointing out that I considered her an important person too, even if she herself did not think so. I looked at the latest signs in her hands and, without overstatement, in a calm, matter-of-fact voice told her about the future I could see for her. I repeated this a second time to make sure that she understood.

I could see that the future had much to offer, once she recovered from her present torment, and that she would once again find happiness in life. Although she had not the remotest idea of remarrying now, she would indeed find a new husband and a new home. I foretold that her future husband would provide well for her and her children, and that they would probably live abroad. Knowing that she was in a precarious position financially, I left money for her, which she kindly accepted. That was the last I saw of her.

Some years later I met someone who knew Margaret, who was able to tell me how she got on subsequently. So that she could pay debts, she sold her house and moved to a temporary home in another district. She divorced her husband and obtained custody of her two children. Eventually she met and married an Englishman whose work took him to the Continent. There Margaret now resides with her children and her new partner. Normality and peace of mind was restored to her and her former agony was a thing of the past.

CHAPTER 11
Career Prospects

THE state of being stagnant or motionless, of being a prey to dullness be it spiritual, mental or material, leads to extinction. Growth, progress, evolution or development are only possible through man using his mind and mental strength in varying ways not limited to merely physical effort. Mental labour is a separate development from physical labour, and can be assisted by the use of spiritual force.

Within the human community are found three categories of worker. The general mass consists of physical workers. Those who recognise the power and range of mind, and are called upon to use this power in planning and further development, are the physico-mental workers. In a class of their own are the purely mental workers, who are capable of using their minds widely and diversely, and who are so talented that success in life seems to come easily for them.

Each one of us can identify our own grade, a group to which we belong according to our own evolutionary development. This state is not haphazardly ordained for us, but is a condition which is our due because we have earned it. As there is a high, middle and a low in animal life in the jungle, so there is a high, middle and low (in the way I have described), in human society.

Certain people have an urge which increases their capacity for methodical, systematic or practical work; and this propensity is often shown in the markings of their palm. Apart from visible signs of capability and determination, a positive mental attitude towards opportunities suited to their purpose, an alert, forward-thinking approach to practical matters is reflected in the highly sensitive recording mechanism which affects hand signs. Conversely, the hand in both its shape and the line markings on the palmar surface will also reflect the less ambitious aspirations of a less gifted person.

The positive aspect of someone's nature, the force of their drive to succeed, the extent to which they could be described as ruthless in pursuit of business opportunities are all factors I have to consider in hand analysis of both physico-mental workers and mental workers.

In moving ahead in time to describe a person's future work pattern where promotion is merited, or where there is some other change in status (from being an employee to being self-employed for instance) clients often express surprise at my interest in their potential. If up to that time they had not considered the possible advantages and challenge of self-employment, then my assessment of their intelligence and potential could lead to a point where it influenced the direction of their future progress. It is not so much a matter of my sowing a seed in the mind, as of my assessment providing insights to future prospects which are already within range but not yet recognised.

Forbidden territory

Some clients, people I would regard as above average intelligence, too often have fixed ideas about the role which they see as right for them. As a result, they tend to overlook possibilities for improving their position, which I am able to detect in my analysis. I can recall two occasions when I described details of clients' work and research which, I was told later, bordered on what could be called 'classified material'.

The first occasion this happened was when I was giving a hand reading with the assistance of clairvoyance, and my mental vision took me aboard a nuclear-powered submarine. I was able to give a description of equipment for which my client was responsible. On the second occasion when talking to a research scientist I described details of integrated circuitry, their colour codes, the raw material involved in the process, and so on. He stopped me at that point, and told me that I was entering a classified zone, so we changed the subject and I continued his reading along more conventional lines.

An inventor came to see me, and looking into the future I was able to describe research involving a new lightweight bullet-proof material for service personnel, and how the material could be adapted for use as light armour. Within a matter of months of that reading I heard that such a material had been discovered earlier by a Government body, which then made some of its findings known to the national press. Within the power of mind everything is possible.

The scale and degree of individual's capacity to express their potential is largely up to them, but timing and opportunity also play an important part in the process. I can recall three separate cases all having one feature in common. This was that I was able to identify a particular talent which each of these clients possess ed in very good measure. I would like to tell you about them.

The first case is that of Kathleen Richmond, a modern young woman concealing considerable creative potential behind the conventional role of happy wife and mother. She had become increasingly restless recently with the predictable routine of domesticated and social life, where she was never expected to play any part more challenging than a supporting role. Her talents clearly were underrated, until she awakened to the fact and began to reassess her situation.

Her visit to me proved to have significant consequences for her later. I could see from her hands that she was a natural organiser, showing originality and enthusiasm in some form of design capacity. Her marriage was happy and secure and giving no cause for worry. She was capable of displaying signs of controlled rebelliousness, at times wishing that she could create a separate world of her own, in which she could express herself, and gain respect and recognition. I did not doubt that she would be highly successful once she began to give expression to her aspirations. But would her husband and family understand her need to step out of her accepted role in their lives?

Kathleen's left hand carried different signs compared with those shown on her right hand. Her left hand showed suppressed originality and independence; sound logic combined with a capacity to reach and sustain decisions; her outgrowing domestication; possessive emotional and sexual relationship with a marriage partner; and a taste for good living, leading to a materialistic outlook and an abiding concern for domestic security. The right hand showed impatience to create opportunities for herself, regardless of assistance which could be provided through her husband and others. These markings confirmed that she was a perfectionist with artistic leanings and a flair for both design and public relations.

Designs on a career

Weighing up the symbolic evidence, I came to the conclusion that Kathleen should create an opportunity for herself, and that she should disregard any criticism of her actions from those close to her. Clairvoyantly I saw a business involving work with fabrics, and I described a number of finished items as I saw them.

Kathleen looked at me attentively, absorbed in what I had to say. I encouraged her to use her business sense and develop ideas which might be exploited, with the assistance of paid help. She said that she could do this. I had confirmed her own thinking in the feasibility of starting a profitable enterprise, and she did not intend to lose sight of any opportunity of the kind we discussed.

Her progress during the next year was remarkable. Having established a business in the manufacture of soft toys, she was able, through contacts and her own capacity for salesmanship and persuasion, to obtain orders from exclusive shops in London and the provinces. It was a marvellous success story, and she has not looked back since.

The second story concerned Madelaine Smithson, a striking-looking woman with a strong outgoing personality to match. Highly sensitive and capable, she nevertheless seemed handicapped by a pessimistic element in her thinking, which dogged her life from time to time, making it extremely difficult to plan effectively.

I saw her frequently over some years, and was always impressed by her adaptability and tenacity, as she seemed always capable of energy and resourcefulness whenever there was a threat to her living standards. Divorced and with two children, one of her chief ambitions was to secure a stable and lasting romantic relationship.

Madelaine's hands were of the artistic type with long, sensitive fingers. Examining them, I could see indications of her possessive and romantic nature, in contrast to her lack of self- confidence in expressing emotion, and slow response to opportunities offering the possibility of new romantic relationships. At the time I felt uneasy for her as this trait in her private life showed little or no change in the foreseeable future. But looking at both palms and relating one to the other, I could see Madelaine's career potential coming to the fore.

The lack of focus in her emotional life had created a vacuum. But it also led in time to a reaction enabling her to direct her energies into more positive channels, leading towards independence. Her hand also displayed a 'writer's fork' which, in turn, could be a factor in her career at some stage in the future. Some form of trigger was needed to set Madelaine on course, and the answer came to me clairvoyantly.

In my mind's eye I saw a cabinet full of exquisite glasses, representing different styles and periods, engraved in delicate patterns and creating a display of refinement and artistry. The glasses were arranged in such a precise, orderly fashion that they could have been in a museum.

Whenever a picture like this forms in my mind, I always describe what I see to my client. At the time of the phenomenon I may not know myself what its true meaning is. I have found that the best thing to do in such circumstances is not to attempt to over-interpret; my rule is simply to explain what I see, as a clearer picture will emerge later. I described my mental picture to Madelaine, and as this followed disclosures from my hand-reading about her future work prospects, it seemed logical to assume that glass of some kind was to feature in her work. At the time, however, this made no sense to her.

In due course, Madelaine was offered a job in the world of antiques, from which she progressed into work of a specialised nature, which involved handling antique glass. She discovered her *forte*. Today she is a leading authority on rare antiques from all over the world, and her work frequently takes her abroad on behalf of certain buyers. Recently she began to compile data about rare glass, with a view to writing a book for connoisseurs and collectors. What began as a visual image in my mind has materialised for Madelaine into a highly successful career.

Never too late

The third case involves a woman over the retirement age who had convinced herself that nothing interesting lay ahead for her, that she had done all that was possible for her to do, and that only decline and death faced her. As she sat in front of me for a reading, she commented, 'Well, young man, I do not know why I am here really. I am too old, and I do not expect that there will be much for you to tell me about my future.' I smiled and answered, 'I hope I will be able to tell you that there is something ahead for you in life. Let me look at your hands and we shall see what comes of it.'

She was gifted with an alert, analytical type of mind, sharp observation and a wide understanding of human nature. Perhaps I should have recognised her name when her appointment was made as she was a well-known author, but I was unaware of this. Ironically, in the early stages of my analysis, I told her she had a gift for writing. She then told me who she was!

I liked her instinctively. Her eyes were bright and clear and missed nothing. She had presence, bearing and a quiet dignity which I found attractive. I imagined her as having the knack of catching the head waiter's eye as soon as she entered an exclusive restaurant. Her hands were of the intuitive type, expressive, agile, flexible and of somewhat elastic texture and their manicure was perfect. They were the hands of a person who had high standards, appreciated comfort and was fortunate always to have people around her who took care of domestic arrangements, thus leaving her free to develop other interests.

Given a task to perform, she was the type of person who could decide quickly which of a number of ways was best suited to the task. Infinite patience was another of her qualities; no issue was too trivial to receive her fullest attention. In her writing this attention to detail was invaluable, as was her meticulousness as a painstaking researcher when preparing material for biographies, histories and the like.

She laughed pleasantly when I told her that although she was a total woman, nevertheless she possessed the logic of a man, for she could hold her own in male company. There had been one main opportunity for marriage, which she had chosen to let pass. In my reading, I saw her writing more books, and I told her that she would embark upon a six-volume work. In this I was not quite correct. What happened was that about that time she was asked by an American publisher to write a book on etiquette in the 1920s. This was such a success that the publisher commissioned her to write a series of five further titles on similar themes.

I told her that she would travel, and she did not seem sure as to whether or not she wanted to travel. Later, it transpired that she went on a world cruise with a companion and, as a result of the success of her books, she went to America and appeared on television. By this time she was close to seventy years of age.

In spiritual terms, palmistically, I could see that she was an 'old soul', and I told her so. This remark struck a special chord for her and, as we conversed, she told me that she believed in reincarnation. She had formed the notion through her sensitivity and varying levels of consciousness that she had lived previously during the reign of Charles I in England, and fought at least one duel with a rapier and had 'pinked' her adversary. At that period in history which she saw as the setting for her past life, she believed herself to have been a man.

In passing, I should say that acceptance of the concept of reincarnation is more important to some people than to others, but nevertheless reincarnation comes within the scope of the power of the mind. Man is mind, the thinker. Man can persist separate and apart from the body, as has been evident through the use of anaesthetics or hypnotism. It seems to me that it follows that if mind can exist even for a moment without the body (remembering that man is a blend of spirit and matter) mind can be seen as both an acknowledgement of spirit, and part of it. This suggests to me that mind can have its own independent form and need not always be integrated with a body. And as I see it there is no logical reason why, divested of a body, mind should not survive throughout eternity. There is nothing ever imagined in mind that does not exist in the universe. Whatever you concentrate on, you draw to yourself.

To return to my client, the accomplished writer. She turned out to be a colourful character and an excellent conversationalist. I was very pleased to see that her later years were full and satisfying, contrary to her bleak expectations. With a little encouragement from me she was able to regain much of her earlier enthusiasm, no doubt because I was able to convince her that her work still was worthwhile, and with a reminder, too, that life was for living.

CHAPTER 12
The Forces of Good and Evil

ALTHOUGH I have always taken an interest in other people, I have also been something of a loner all my life, a detached observer noting all who pass by my window. I believe it is this sense of detachment which helps me to be objective and impartial. Whether my client is an ordinary person or someone famous makes no difference to me in my task of providing a hand analysis, but I may find the life of an airline pilot more interesting than that of a politician.

I also attach no importance to the sort of prestige that may be acquired by name-dropping; people who do so are, in my opinion, shallow and of little account. Wisdom may often be learnt from an ordinary man more readily than from an educated one. People who are interesting are not necessarily likeable. How a self-made millionaire gained his fortune when he began life with nothing would, I think, be of interest; but the millionaire himself may not have an amiable personality.

I remember the day I had a mercenary as a client. I found the man interesting, but the nature of his work did not appeal to me. His hands were of the practical kind, but the complex type. The palm was square, the fingers short. The palmar surface showed few lines, but those visible were strong and vital in their expression. The texture of his skin was coarse. The thumbs tended to be inflexible and were shorter than average in length.

I had described his current restlessness of mood and said that he was being offered work abroad, when he volunteered the information that he was a mercenary. He looked back at me with wide open eyes which seldom blinked; his hair was cut short all over his head, as is often advocated when working in a hot climate, and it may well have been a requirement in his job. He said he hoped to be going to Southern Africa soon.

His hands showed that romantically and emotionally he was searching for that satisfaction which comes from sharing a lasting love. A romance he had come to depend on in the past had either let him down or simply burnt itself out. My assessment showed that, of his own choosing, he would always have two women in his life: one probably a lasting love of sorts; the second, a temporary mistress, who would be replaced by another and then another for as long as it suited him.

The mind of a mercenary

When the reading was over, we talked for a while before he left. I wanted to learn more of what might be termed the typical mentality of a mercenary. 'Let us suppose that you and I were close friends, and that through changing circumstances we found ourselves supporting opposing political parties,' I said. 'And suppose that for some reason I was in the way, and a contract was put out to have me killed. And let us suppose, too, that you were given the job of getting rid of me. Would you do it?'

Without hesitation he replied, 'Yes.' He looked me straight in the eye. 'But as we were friends,' he added, 'as a favour to you, I would shoot you here.' With the index finger of one hand he pointed at a spot above his upper lip. He explained: 'When you shoot at somebody, if you are aiming at the heart, there is no guarantee that the first bullet will hit the intended area, because it can be deflected by bone, muscle, veins or arteries which direct the projectile elsewhere. Bullets come out of strange places on a human target. So, as a favour to you, I would make sure you did not suffer and that it would be a quick finish.'

I thanked him. He rose to leave and his athletic elegance caught my eye, the movements cat-like, economical, automatic. His slim, muscular body did not have a trace of unnecessary fat. We shook hands, and he left.

Ambition never satisfied

In an effort to adapt to a hostile world most people try to be successful in their chosen career. But for some the objective of being 'king of the pile' is taken too seriously, while others whose ambitious drives can never be satisfied, no matter how much success they attain, continue to seek further stimulation in pursuits of even more spectacular achievement.

To avoid stagnation is one thing, but never to know when to stop is a recipe for permanent discontent. In such cases wealth, achievement, distinction do not lead to happiness and a sense of stability, because for them success contains within itself the kernel of destruction. No doubt many of these supercharged success seekers realise too late that life could have been happier with fewer accomplishments and more time to enjoy living! Yet society encourages them to keep up the myth that the pursuit is everything, and so they are under continual pressure to excel. Anything less, or failure itself, could make them bitter and cruel; and indeed, no-one accepts failure easily.

Capacity to love

One such man, having achieved considerable success, but trapped in an unhappy marriage from which he could not free himself, came to see me in an attempt to find peace and stability in his romantic life. It seemed clear from the beginning that his emotional intensity militated against this, because whenever there were difficulties in his romantic life, he quickly found solace in business success.

He had a brilliant mind, but it was not in his nature to be conventional or to live simply. His great tragedy was that either he had lost the capacity to love, or that he was still trying to rediscover it. In looking at his palm I could see that there was another woman in his life who posed a direct challenge to his own wife. His present desire for stability was prompted by his involvement with his current mistress. Nevertheless, however valuable this relationship could be proved to be for him, he would feel himself driven to sidestep and evade commitment in the long run. The energy I saw within his hand directed my attention to his business affairs. It was an intoxicating world of speculative projects, and I could foresee him embarking on a new venture outside of his successful construction business.

When the hand-reading was completed, we went into another room for coffee prepared by Cis, my dear lady companion. In a more relaxed setting the man who until then had scarcely spoken, appearing withdrawn and rather secretive, began to talk. His girl-friend, who had brought him for the consultation, also joined in the conversation. He expressed surprise at the accuracy of my assessment; and said he had been very sceptical about seeing me. In the discussion, when he was asked about his romantic future, he was diplomatic but uninformative. He did everything but give a direct answer, other than to say that he knew what he should do, and that time would tell ...

Then he made an unusual revelation. He told me that during the 1939-1945 war he had been engaged in the intelligence service. Part of his job then was to interrogate prisoners or suspects in order to obtain information, assess its value, and decide how much they were concealing.

I gathered from this that my client had been some sort of spy-catcher. The training he received for this work had given him considerable insight into human beings and their motivation. So as he absorbed what I had to reveal during my analysis, he in turn was analysing me. He looked for give-away nerve points on my face, neck and elsewhere, which would have been activated had I been under strain at any time during the hand-reading or had I been lying to him. His search drew a blank; he found no such evidence. He had been using a technique similar to that used today by Government inspectors when observing travellers at passport and Customs checkpoints.

The fact that I had not asked any questions had intrigued him, and the accuracy of my reading had taken him by surprise. He was not used to anyone, let alone a stranger, knowing that much about him. The following day his girl-friend telephoned to say he had stayed up until the early hours of the morning talking about his experience and going over the details of my analysis, point by point.

I have no doubt that this man will succeed in most undertakings of a business designed to support him in the world of high living to which he has become accustomed. I doubt whether the true depth of his emotional feelings can be ascertained, so true tranquility will continue to elude him. I could see his romantic life punctuated by a series of mistresses, but the abiding love he wished for would somehow remain elusive.

Another client, David Mortimer, was an interesting person who worked in electronics. His hand was of the sensitive type with a long narrow palm and long tapering fingers. The palmar surface was covered by a large number of fine lines. I did not see his career lasting. I foresaw that external conditions would involve domestic and environmental changes, which would compel him to undertake work modifications in the future. David felt insecure and was apt to be moody. At times he was conscious of lacking inside himself a sense that he really belonged anywhere. He was dissatisfied with his own performance in life, feeling that he had not achieved anything worthwhile. When feeling particularly low he would seek reassurance and then, as likely as not, he would resent the involvement of a counsellor and any reassurance given. He came to see me more than once, and I always felt a vague uneasiness about the circumstances of his future, although I could not pinpoint what it was that made me apprehensive for him.

Turning the tables

During one visit to me, he disclosed that he had made investigations about me. His reason for checking me out, so he said, was that he usually had a pigeon-hole for everyone, but having met me for the first time had to admit that I did not fit into any category that he could think of. His investigation disclosed nothing amiss and his face-to-face analysis of my character also drew a blank. Some time afterwards he was convicted on a charge of handling stolen goods. This explained the break in his career that I saw marked upon his hand.

On another occasion when I was using my clairvoyant vision during a reading given to a businessman in the building trade, I felt compelled to describe how he was being cheated by a member of the staff. This involved the falsification of estimates and accounts. My client, whose name was Bill Tyson, refused to believe me at first, and so did not act upon what I had revealed. As a result he continued to be out of pocket for longer than necessary through the malpractice I had described.

Eventually, with financial losses continuing on a regular and virtually commonplace basis, he became concerned to such an extent that he took heed of my observations and set a trap for the culprit. The guilty person was exposed very quickly and dismissed. This particular employee felt himself to be a failure and was no doubt bitter and envious of the success of his employer, who had always treated him with fairness and generosity.

A similar case was that of another business client, to whom I revealed that a member of his staff had been purloining some of the stock for a considerable time. He smiled when he heard this, and asked me how on earth I knew. Subsequently, through my confirmation of the dishonest practice, my client had the incentive to set a plan in motion which caught the thief in the act.

In life we find that signs which are visible on the surface reflect undercurrents which are invisible below the surface. The manner of the working of good and evil has many similarities; it is the end products which are in direct opposition. Clairvoyant vision is an extension of the senses, a more sophisticated level of thought force. The law which rules the physical applies also to the spiritual. The Absolute also applies Its own law unto Itself, 'As is above, so is below.'

CHAPTER 13
First Impressions

DURING the time I have been working as a palmist clairvoyant I have never felt it necessary to advertise myself. A business card can serve its purpose for clients, but I believe that a sound reputation is the best means of making oneself known. In this way the word is spread and new clients seek me out.

The closest I come to advertising is by lecturing, but that is not restricted to the subject of palmistry alone. One of my lecture engagements took me to Dagenham, an industrial town east of London, where my subject for the evening was the history of palmistry and its influence today.

Cis, my lady companion, accompanied me. On the way to Dagenham she said, 'This particular audience will either like you, or throw their bread rolls at you.' The function was a club dinner with the speaker for 'dessert'. On such occasions I eat sparingly; it would not do for the speaker to nod off while giving his talk.

The venue was a public house and the function was held in a large room at one side of the building. It was a well-organised affair, with the audience seated at connecting tables arranged in the form of the capital letter E. I stood on a spot-lit rostrum facing the three prongs of the E and the gallery of viewers ranged across most of the full width of the room.

My talks involve audience participation, which is very popular. This follows my description of the position and meaning of the principal lines to be found upon the hand, with illustrations on a blackboard which I use for the purpose.

On this occasion, when the time came for me to give some

demonstrations of hand-reading, I asked those at the rear of the audience to hold up their hands as if they were being held at gunpoint. I remained standing at the rostrum. I find that I can read hands at a distance of 20 feet (6 metres) or thereabouts. Selecting one person for a reading, I told the remainder to lower their hands and relax. Then I began an analysis.

This is obviously somewhat different from the manner in which I conduct a private reading. In lecture demonstrations there is not time to keep the audience waiting. I draw my information from the shape of the hand as well as the palm itself. These two domains are known by their respective names; to recap, the study of the lines of the palm is known as cheiromancy, whereas the study of the meaning derived from the shapes of the hands and fingers is known as cheirognomy. When lecturing and giving demonstrations I cannot openly disclose some of the information I am able to detect. For example, the gentleman in the fifth row may be married yet having an affair; I can be aware of this through my reading of his hand - but would not tell him so in front of others!

Once, following a lecture, I spoke to a man in the audience, making sure to speak so quietly that nothing could be overheard. He was rather vain and conceited. I told him that although he was married, he was having an affair and was planning to leave his wife, whom I perceived to be ignorant of the blow about to fall. He was not at all pleased with my revelation. 'What you have just seen, you have no right to know,' he retorted. My answer was a smile.

Audience participation

Practice in reading hands at a distance evolved during my early days of lecturing when I used to mix with the audience. People would crowd round me eagerly and without discipline, making it very difficult to concentrate on an analysis. My ability to read hands at a distance solved the problem. It is an expertise which can take the audience unawares, as there are always those in a group who are intensely curious about other people's affairs but very reluctant to face scrutiny themselves.

At the Dagenham meeting, when I had completed some demonstrations which were well received, I turned to a woman seated at one side, not far from the rostrum. As she held up both hands, I described her interest in the welfare of children, her own and others, and mentioned that there would soon be an addition to the family. This brought good-natured laughter from the audience, from the tone of which it appeared that they knew something about the lady in question which I did not know.

A wag in the audience called out, 'Her husband will be interested to know about it; he has been done, he has had the operation.' Further laughter rippled around the room, with the woman herself joining in self-consciously. 'I do not change what I see,' I said. 'There will be an addition to the family, and everything will be conducted in a proper and decent fashion.' Having nothing else to say to her, I turned to give a reading to another member of the audience.

My talk and demonstrations ran over time as the audience was eager for more revelations. Having done their duty, the pub staff grew irritable. Anxious for me to be gone so that they could go to their homes, they began flashing lights on and off. At about the third attempt they succeeded in getting their message over to the audience, and the meeting came to an end.

As people dispersed, the woman for whom I had predicted an addition to the family came to speak to me. She explained that although her husband had had a vasectomy so that he could not father any more children, they had in addition to the children of their marriage, a young coloured foster child. Their love for this child was such that they had applied for an adoption order, which would make the child theirs permanently. I thanked her for telling me this, adding that I did not think the adoption would be opposed.

This example proved to me once again that with clairvoyance - whether used in private or public - it is important for the medium to hold mentally to whatever first impression is received. The medium's message may not be understood initially by the client; and there will be some people who reject the message; but when practised correctly, clairvoyance is both accurate and reliable in most instances.

Years of indecision

I recall an earlier case which illustrates this point. When I gave a private consultation to Amanda Kelsey, I found her hand difficult to interpret. When my examination focused on her marriage and private life, her hand showed that she had been married-divorced, married-divorced, married-divorced - all to the same man. When I told her this and said that it did not make sense to me, she laughed delightedly, and in turn explained what I had seen, which was correct.

Amanda was a lively girl with an all too trusting nature, one of those people who are eternal givers, and whose hearts so often rule their heads. Impetuous and impatient, she married while still in her teens but soon discovered that the relationship between herself and her husband was one with a strong love-hate element. Tensions and dissatisfactions led her when still barely twenty to consider divorce, but this course was averted through an emotional reconciliation.

There were three surviving children of the marriage, and in loving and caring for them Amanda was a much more dependable parent than her husband. Later she discovered him being unfaithful, and once again considered divorce action, only to withdraw her application at the last minute. Three years later their marriage had run into further storms and the couple were now living separate lives. Never at any time had legal action been initiated by Amanda's husband. She now saw that responsibility for the future of the marriage was up to her alone.

In the event of the third serious crisis, a stage was reached where a decree *nisi* was prepared (a decree which eventually becomes *absolute* unless cause is shown why this should not be permitted) and the only thing now needed was her signature. But at the eleventh hour her heart ruled her head once again and she could not bring herself to sever the marriage ties.

I was used to seeing Amanda as a slim, attractive woman with a lively, carefree attitude to life. Then she came one day, and she had changed so much in her personality and appearance that I had difficulty in recognising her as the same woman. Gone was the vivacity and slender figure. The woman before me was subdued, irritable and overweight. She was also very depressed.

Changed personality

By the time Amanda visited me again, she had recovered her figure, and much of her former vitality. And the line markings on her palms had changed. The area relating to marriage reflected some of her former ambiguity with regard to divorce and making a final break with her husband. This time, however, there was no longer any doubt in her mind as to what she should do. And although long overdue, the divorce which she should have obtained when she was much younger, left her free to enjoy life once again with a degree of self-confidence not known previously.

CHAPTER 14
Family Backgrounds

OUR early years are vitally important, not only because of the influences which can be observed to be at work in developing strength and character, but even more so in developing the unseen strengths beneath the surface, within the individual's emotional depths. This period, I believe, lasts from birth until the child reaches the age of seven years. For the more sensitive type of person, a receptive mind, and a sense of being understood and belonging to those close to them, are likely to be of greater significance than early indoctrination in the ways of worldly success.

Once a stable background has been established for the child, the pursuit of attainment can follow on naturally within the range of individual competence. A man placed in solitary confinement could begin that existence with limited knowledge. Yet in a positive state of mind he could develop an interest in learning; and through the fact of being solitary with no distractions, he could make academic progress. However, this achievement would serve only a limited purpose if that man could not share his thoughts and his learning with others, for despite his attainments he would still be denied the gift of being able to communicate. This lack could lead to emotionally damaging inhibitions and complexes which the person concerned would have to learn to overcome or live with, while making the best of their life-style.

Early training should not be centred solely on preparations to launch the child towards a life of his own. It should also include a blending of the human qualities of love and closeness and harmony to nurture the emotional life of the individual. It is only through such a full experience that a person can begin properly to understand for themselves what love is, and its role in relationships.

Any insecurity or emotional instability experienced in a person's early life is recorded upon the palm. This often is an important factor in any analysis which takes into account symptoms of cause and effect. I am just as much interested in a client's beginnings as I am in his or her situation at the time of a first visit to me, or in their future circumstances.

Some time ago I gave a consultation to a young German student from Stuttgart, with the aid of an interpreter. During my analysis he expressed surprise that from the lines on his hand I could tell that he did not know the identity of his real parents. He was rather self-conscious over this matter, as he had been adopted. One legacy of this early set-back was a certain guardedness concerning his personal life and self-image, which would probably remain with him for the rest of his life.

This young man's highly sensitive nature made him an incessant worrier, to the extent that I found it necessary to warn him about his future health. I told him that a stomach weakness could lead to an ulcer requiring medical treatment. About one year later, he asked a friend to write to me from Germany confirming that he was then in hospital recovering from the effects of a stomach ulcer. The condition may have been due predominantly to physical causes, but I also think that his worries over his past contributed to the illness.

Genetic factors

Disturbances in early home life will show up on the hand, as will an affinity between the client and one parent more than the other. A special affinity for one parent may be the result of genetic factors, as well as being evidence of the closeness of emotions, mind and spirit - a kinship of particular value to the subject. Illigitimacy and other social conditions can be registered upon the hands of both parent and child. A woman's hand can show that she bore a child while married, but sometimes other features of the palm can indicate that the father of the child is not necessarily the woman's husband. An additional clue in circumstances of this nature is the effect it produces on the child. This may be reflected in its pattern of reactions towards early environment, and in the subjective attitude towards its own origin. As to who the child's father is, that is a secret a woman can carry with her to the grave.

Here is another instance where such information may be sought. Let us suppose that a single woman had affairs with two men at a time when she became pregnant. She may then want to decide which of the two men she wishes to marry, though she may still not know which man is the father of her child. Should the man she marries not be the child's father, then this fact would be shown upon the hand.

Divided loyalties

The case of Anthony Henderson is an interesting example of mental awareness bordering on a psychic state of mind, associated with a young man's inner certainty that the man he called 'Dad' was not in fact his real father. Confirmation was eventually provided unexpectedly when it was time for him to choose a career. Anthony's natural inclination pointed him in one direction, while family loyalties pulled him in another direction. The lack of affinity between him and his supposed father increased to such a degree that his recurring suspicions about his paternity assumed a new importance in his life. And he began a search for information to support his view and help him to locate his real father. He knew that his mother had been married only once.

Anthony had a sharp, analytical mind and tended at times to be remote and withdrawn. But his quiet charm, air of distinction and expressive brown eyes were an irresistible attraction to the opposite sex. He was not a womaniser and remained loyal to his marriage vows. Nevertheless, there were women whose attempts at seduction seemed promising until they came up against an immovable barrier of indifference, which left them with the impression that he was lost in a world of his own.

I was impressed, when I first looked at his hands, at the practical ability clearly indicated on his palms. His hands were strong, pliable, with long, moderately tapering fingers. His skin was smooth and clean. The lines on his hands showed extreme sensitivity, sentimentality, an interest in the ways of the modern world, sound logic deriving from experience and intuition, and practical skills in the field of public relations.

I saw that if Anthony tried to maintain a balance between his chosen loyalties on the one side and his desire for independence on the other, he would end up in the unhappy situation where the wishes of others always took precedence over opportunities for his own success. He came to me a number of times over a period of some years, and I was able to help in shaping his future ideas as well as by giving practical guidance with regard to his finances and home affairs. As time passed we also became close friends, a rare occurrence in my work because of my self-imposed discipline, which demands a certain detachment from my clients.

Anthony worked in the City of London for a foreign firm. A point came where he was aware of changes going on around him, which did not affect his working position at first, but involved him eventually. There was a certain amount of pressure associated with the responsibilities of his job and the business policies he was called upon to implement. His acute, sensitive nature reacted against these pressures, and he became increasingly unhappy with his job. Nor did he find it encouraging to see people with long service with the organisation being transferred to another branch at short notice, or even posted abroad.

A man could be told on a Friday that he was expected to start work at another location by 9 a m the following Monday. He might be transferred from London to Belgium. If he disagreed with the order he faced dismissal, because the firm's employment contract required that employees agree to being sent anywhere on the firm's business. In practice, any inconvenience such a transfer caused a man's wife and family was treated with indifference by the management. Where a marriage problem arose as a result of the transfer, and a solution could not be achieved within a prescribed time, the bank would insist on the employee's allegiance and offer help with the costs of a divorce. With the bank, business always came first. In addition, its trading was moving towards the Far East and away from London, its original overseas trading headquarters. This then was Anthony Henderson's working background.

Reaching a turning point

I saw and analysed two separate developments in Anthony's life: the direction of his career, and the impact on his sensitive nature of his family's attitude towards him. It was at this point during a reading that I told him of my feeling that the man assumed to be his father was not necessarily his true father, and that I could not see an affinity between them. He listened thoughtfully, and then said he agreed with my observation.

The solution to his dilemma as to which was more important to him, freedom or family loyalty, lay in his capacity to develop his career regardless of criticism from others. Furthermore, he knew that his wife would stand by him in whatever choice he made. He also wanted to find out for himself if his doubts concerning his father's identity were justified.

I saw two career changes in his hand, both involving home moves. Anthony gave in notice to leave his company when working conditions there became too much for him. (Had he remained in that job the pressures he was under would have made him ill.) He then took on a temporary job of a different kind, while waiting for another opening in import/export. After some time, during which I gave him consultations, he was offered a job overseas.

Arrangements were made for the family to move abroad. His home in England was sold. Before he left, his mother gave him some family items of sentimental value, including photographs. One of the photographs provided firm support for his belief that his mother's husband was not his real father. Until now he had never spoken to his mother about his doubts. Although he felt instinctively that his guess was correct, his mother did not offer any information on the matter. So he decided that it was best not to disturb her by asking questions, though he was convinced that the photograph supplied the missing link in the mystery of his parentage.

The photograph in question showed a group of men standing side by side. Close to the man his mother had married was another man who was a close friend of the family. The physical resemblance between Anthony and this other man was unmistakable. There were obvious similarities in the shape of the head, shape and style of the hands, facial expression, set of the eyes, and physical posture. But the man was believed to have been killed in action during the 1939-1945 world war.

Anthony's wife showed me the photograph during a weekend visit, and without prompting I picked out the two men, and said I thought that the second man was Anthony's real father. Unknown to me, some time earlier the same day, Cis, my lady companion, had been shown the picture; and without prompting of any kind, had reached the same conclusion. Soon afterwards, Anthony and his wife left England for a new life abroad.

Due to the nature of my work I should not be surprised by unexpected occurrences and coincidences. Yet it struck me as curious that scarcely a fortnight after I was shown the photograph by my client, Anthony Henderson, I should be confronted with a similar case, that of a journalist, Julian Thomas.

Masculine intuition

Thomas's hand was of the practical type, and what was particularly interesting about it was the marked line of intuition, which is not often found on a man's hand. Intuition is a quality more commonly attributed to women. Highly sensitive and incurably romantic, Thomas - like Henderson - was a loner, but his intuitive sense was strong and active. For some years he had seen little of his family as he seemed to have less in common with them as time passed, and his work took him farther afield. His progress in life showed no trace of family influence.

The patterns of his early development were reflected upon his hand, showing key points in his life from his twenty-eighth year onwards. During my analysis I referred to some aspects of his family background. When I said that he took after his mother, more than his father, he produced a photograph once given to him by his father. His mother had died whilst he was quite young, and his father had since remarried. I drew a parallel between his circumstances and those of Anthony Henderson. Here again was photographic evidence that the man assumed to be the parent was not the real father.

I told him what I considered to be the truth as to his origin, and afterwards found that I had merely confirmed his own view on the matter. I asked him whether this made any difference as to how he felt about himself or his family. He replied with sincerity that he would never condemn anyone in a situation of this kind. But he was interested in discovering his origins, and this knowledge put family issues in a clearer perspective for him. He saw no reason to make any changes in his relationships, but decided that there was no longer any need for him to become involved in the life his so-called father now had. He thanked me for putting his mind at ease, and we parted in a friendly manner.

Despite the many years I have been a palmist clairvoyant, my readings never follow a set pattern. This is because I do not consciously plan at the start of a consultation the direction in which I think the reading should go. Keeping an open mind, I look for indications on the palm upon which a prediction can be made. I am sometimes as surprised as clients at what can be revealed about them, very often to the good.

One evening a client who had been to see me a number of times brought her mother and mother's friend for a hand-reading. The mother, Nancy Newbolt, chose to have her reading first. She seemed shy as she sat opposite me, leaning forward with both palms outstretched, head down, her eyes scanning the lines on the palmar surface with no apparent trace of understanding. When I spoke to her, she kept her head down, with her gaze fixed as though unaware of her surroundings. Her expression was serious as she listened to my analysis.

I told her that I could see two men in her past life, each appearing at different stages. There was an early marriage which produced one child. Following that, she was emotionally involved with someone whom I described as 'the second man in her life'. I saw that this was an important relationship for her, that it was like a second marriage, but produced no children. She nodded in agreement.

Lifting the barrier

I knew little about Nancy despite having her daughter as a regular client. I preferred it that way, as it meant that my mind was free from preconceived impressions. To me, the client is an individual, who must always come first, regardless of any knowledge I may already have of close relatives.

It seemed to me that Nancy's main problem was the barrier created by her natural reserve, which made it very difficult to discover what went on in her mind, what she felt or, for that matter, wanted out of life. Her hands showed in their line formations that her past life had not been an easy one. She achieved nothing without determined personal effort. No help came from relatives or other family connections, perhaps because she was too independent to approach them. She had suffered deep emotional strain which contributed to her tendency to take a reserved and defensive attitude towards the world. Some would call her 'deep'.

Making a closer study of her hand, with particular attention to the formation of her heart line and other pointers, I caught a glimpse of her as she was in her youth, romantic, carefree, optimistic. So I looked back into her past and recalled for her how joyfully she had reacted to courtship in those days. This contrasted sharply with her present life, in which she was without a partner, which worried her, although she was too proud to admit it to a soul. I felt that she wished to find a romantic partner with whom she could share a happy and harmonious future, but she lacked the self-confidence necessary to make a new beginning. Nor did she appear to have any practical ideas as to how best to begin her quest.

As I described her past life, and depicted her as a once vibrant, fun-loving young woman, Nancy began to laugh with good humour. Her serious expression fell away; her eyes lost their look of cautious woefulness and began to sparkle in the light, radiating warmth and vitality. Her laughter removed the barriers which she had erected at the start of my analysis. For over half an hour, someone had talked to her about herself, making her the centre of attention. The effect of this was to raise her spirits, and she felt no embarrassment in having a stranger telling her truths about herself. We exchanged smiles and enjoyed mental rapport.

At the time I had no idea how quickly a change was to be made in Nancy's life as a result of my revelations. This came about the same evening while I was giving a reading to Nancy's woman friend. In an adjoining room a conversation took place between Nancy and her daughter in the presence of my lady companion, Cis.

Cis had noticed that, before the reading, Nancy's manner had been reserved and she did not have much to say. When she returned to the room after the hand-reading, Cis offered her coffee, and in the course of conversation asked her if she was pleased with the reading. Nancy replied that she was happy about it, and that she was surprised at the accuracy of my description of her past life.

When Nancy visited the bathroom, her daughter said to Cis, 'He must have said something good to my mother, she seems so changed - in fact she seems like an altogether different person. In all the years I've known my mother, I have never seen her so talkative and jolly. She has always been so serious.'

Her mother came back into the room. Conversation resumed and, turning to her daughter, Nancy referred to some event in the younger woman's childhood. 'I remember that,' the daughter rejoined. 'Dad was there.' Her father had been dead for many years and Nancy's daughter was now in her thirties, married, with two children of her own.

Nancy looked at her and suddenly exclaimed, 'Oh, but that was not your father.' Not understanding, her daughter replied, 'I am talking about Dad; you know, Dad, who was with us then.' 'Yes,' said Nancy, 'I know. But I am telling you that he was not your father.'

Pale and visibly shocked, her daughter asked, 'What do you mean?' 'Well, I have been wanting to tell you this for many years, but I have never been able to bring myself to do so,' Nancy said. Looking round at the room with its open fireplace, old oak beams and tranquil decor, she went on, 'It must be something to do with the atmosphere of this place, that I feel I can tell you now.'

'Who then is my father?' the daughter asked, as she rallied from the shock. Nancy's story went back many years. When still very young, she married and gave birth to a daughter. Sadly, the marriage did not last. While her daughter was still a baby, Nancy's husband walked out, leaving his wife and child. Modernists must bear in mind that these events took place over thirty years ago, in a world of very different attitudes and social values. With little or no help available from social services, Nancy had to find a means of supporting herself and her child. She moved into a rented flat, and started a job when she found someone to mind her daughter during working hours. There were no other resources available; Nancy had to keep them both.

During this period Nancy was introduced to a man serving in the Royal Navy, with whom she began courtship. He wished to marry Nancy, but he already had a wife who would not let him have a divorce. He did not want to part from Nancy, so it was agreed that he would live with her whenever he was on leave.

Nancy changed her surname to his and became known as Mrs. Newbolt. Neighbours assumed that the couple were married, and this spared Nancy discomfort and embarrassment, as in those days it was socially unacceptable for a couple to 'live in sin'. As a result of this arrangement, Nancy brought up her daughter to call the man she lived with, 'Daddy'.

Sadly, Nancy's lover was taken ill suddenly and died, while away from home. As only the man's legal wife was notified, Nancy did not know about his death until just before the funeral, when she heard the news from an acquaintance. So came to an end a happy period with the man of her choice. The man's legal wife inherited all his estate, and Nancy received nothing. Her daughter was at that time a teenager.

With the weight of her secret lifted after so many years, Nancy felt relieved and happy to have confided in her daughter at last. Although clearly shocked by these revelations, the daughter loved her mother dearly. She said later that what had surprised her most was her mother's failure to inform her of the facts earlier.

In the region of the palm where markings known as 'marriage lines' are to be found, Nancy's hand showed two marriage marks. It takes skill to distinguish between a so-called marriage line which may relate to a short-lived affair; the type of mark denoting a 'trial marriage', where a couple choose to live together on a long- term basis, and the true marriage line which confirms the more conventional partnership. Marriage marks appear naturally on the hands of both men and women, so interpretation of their meaning needs to be worked out carefully in each case.

Although not officially recognised, Nancy's bond with her lover expressed such abiding love and affinity that the lines on her hand registered their union as of more significance than that of some couples who have taken solemn vows in a wedding ceremony. And the closer rapport which has grown up between Nancy, her daughter and her grandchildren, since her revelation, does much to compensate Nancy for the struggle of her early years.

CHAPTER 15
Exercising Free-will

CONSIDER for a moment, free-will, and what it implies: the power of self-determination; liberty of choice; or, if you prefer, freedom of the will from restraint. It is an important element of our personality and consciousness, closely allied to liberty itself. Though available to us all, it is not always fully understood. It is used, I believe, only to a limited extent in the majority of people's lives.

The restrictions militating against a person's use of free-will can be numerous. These include self-doubt; an existing commitment to a way of life which imposes its own limitations; duties and loyalties to family causes or even lost causes, which may seem unavoidable but are not always in the individuals' best interests. In such circumstances liberty gives way to convention, and free-will is limited in its range of effectiveness.

The concept of liberty is so important that it is seen by a great many people as something worth fighting and dying for. Yet given liberty, some people would choose instead a mode of life so restrictive as to undermine free-will and the quality of life itself.

The palm can register three salient factors relevant to an individual's personality and life history. These are free-will, hand-speed, and timing of events. Hand-speed, as I have mentioned earlier, relates to a person's awareness and increasingly evident potential in terms of ability to meet future challenges. Timing is a vital quality, whether controlled by the individual, or directed by external events linked with the individual. Lost opportunities remain lost. Every aim or purpose has its own allotted time-span, and the best use must be made of it. Where someone fails to use such an opportunity, it is his or her own responsibility if the eventual outcome turns out to be less advantageous than it could have been.

The gift of happiness

I recall the case of Claire Ashenden, a client of whom I was particularly fond. I knew Claire for many years. She was one of those beautiful souls whose warmth and vitality had an unusually contagious quality, marking her out as an inspiration to others. She was a shrewd observer of human nature, with a sufficient depth of understanding to qualify her as a natural advisor and counsellor. Yet while her intelligence won admiration, she had a stubborn streak which occasionally let her down.

Although she had travelled widely, Claire chose as her home, London, the Gemini city, where she enjoyed a good social life and could indulge her love of opera, ballet and the theatre.

She was interested in palmistry and studied it. We met often and became close friends. Occasionally she would ask me to look at her hands. Quite soon after our first meeting, my reading pointed to a dilemma which was adversely affecting her progress in life. For the most part her natural talent and ability could carry her forward with distinction. Her social life was a success. But her impressive achievements so far, and the rich promise which the future held, were being put at risk by an obstacle in her path - her ambivalent attitude to divorce.

I saw that if she were to escape now from an unhappy marriage, she would still be young enough to plan a new life without lowering her living standards. I described the abuses she had endured in her marriage. I said although she might still love her husband he had chosen not to make her happy. Therefore it was necessary, in my view, for her to seek a divorce. But I warned her that due to her husband's influence in certain quarters, the divorce would be socially embarrassing, and that a scandal involving her husband might be exposed. Yet despite these problems it was essential that she consider taking action to regain her liberty.

I remember the serious expression on Claire's face as I told her this. Looking directly into my face, she said she was in complete agreement with me, and that she should divorce her husband because of his adultery. Between that day and the time when she eventually decided to take legal action, there was a lapse of ten years. Had she obtained a divorce when I first counselled her to act, she would have fared better.

By her own choosing to delay such a length of time before a divorce, Claire was having to cope with the problem when she was ten years older. And in the long interval she had also lost the drive and incentive needed to take proper advantage of what would have been her fair share of the marital home. So the enigma remained and her life-style suffered accordingly. It seemed as though the gains she was allowed to make in life by the time she reached middle age were from then onward to be denied her.

When the divorce was granted, it ended twenty-two years of a marriage in which there were no children. Claire set about fending for herself, and found a job. Barely a year later Roger, her former husband, died suddenly. Had she remained married to him, Claire would have been the sole beneficiary of his estate. As it was, it took two-and-a-half years for his legal affairs to be settled, by which time Claire was in ill health, suffering from overwork and the bitterness of knowing that her financial circumstances were far less favourable than they could have been. Nor did it improve matters for her when the ex-wife and children of Roger's first marriage successfully claimed part of his estate.

The London house in which Claire lived was registered as a company house, and so on Roger's death this had to be sold. Claire then moved to her second home, a country property after the style of an old farmhouse, which was costly to maintain. Burdens of this sort wore her down further, so that at times she would no longer have had enough physical strength to go on, were it not for her courage and stubbornness. She ignored advice that she should give up her job and sell one or two possessions, so that she could live reasonably on the proceeds. As she owned many fine antiques and some valuable paintings, this seemed an obvious solution to her immediate problems.

Continuing ill health obliged her to give up her job, eventually. The country house was sold and Claire lived with friends for a time before returning to London. The divorce settlement from Roger was minimal, and before she was able to find a permanent home of her own, her illness became worse and she had to go into hospital. Two years later, after three operations, she died of cancer - a sad conclusion to a life in which there had been so much vitality.

All her life Claire had been a tremendous giver, whose interests and enthusiasm found expression in great generosity towards others. Yet the living style she could have expected in her later life was denied her. Her possessions were scattered in the safekeeping of others during her long period of stress and ill health. Never once had I seen her lose her dignity; and hearing her happy laughter in a garden or over a dining table one could not fail to respond and share the moment with her. The ability to communicate happily and to be an inspiration to others within her circle was a gift she could use to perfection - though sadly not in her marriage.

The facility to switch easily from one task to another equally demanding, calls for a special talent in itself. This talent is registered upon the palm in the marking known as the head line, which shows the potential for versatility and enterprise in a person's working life, where such qualities can lead to a desired goal. The time-scale associated with such an opportunity may be critical, since it so often happens that the response to a challenge can be made only within a set period. If through hesitation, doubt, or for any reason, the person in such a situation fails to take advantage of the opportunity or offer within the prescribed period, no amount of talent can compensate for the delay.

Occasionally, I meet someone for whom such mischance has made all the difference between phenomenal success and dismal failure in the direction of a career. Quite often the explanation is that they were held back by existing commitments which left little time for new challenges, or to consider the choices available. The preferred choice in such cases could be strongly indicated on the individual's hand, but the necessity to comply with a precise time-scale underlines the risk of failure through running out of time.

This was the type of problem I saw reflected in the hands of Dave Armstrong, a versatile craftsman, with strong hands, and well-formed fingers, which were straight and, in palmistic terms, square-ended. He could produce effective and artistic work, using most materials, including brick, stone, wood and modern plastics.

Dave had strong feelings which he tended not to disclose, except in the company of close friends or new acquaintances who shared his views. Far from being a sceptic, he believed in the power of mind and nature forces, but nevertheless demanded proof wherever possible when encountering new sources of knowledge.

I remember an occasion when Dave came to me for a consultation. He had been quite satisfied with my prediction during a previous consultation. But when he came to my home to arrange another appointment and found me busy in my garden, he greeted me with a challenge. 'Leonard,' he said, 'I want another reading. You were one hundred per cent correct the last time, but that was luck, a fluke. No way will you be right this time.'

I had been weeding, and my hands daubed with soil from the garden, but hearing his challenge, I said on impulse that I would give his hands a brief examination there and then. He allowed me to do so, while Cis stood nearby watching.

Clearing my mind I concentrated on both of his outstretched hands, although I did not touch them. A minute passed, and we stood transfixed while I said nothing. Then I spoke: 'You are going to change your job,' I said. My statement took the wind out of his sails. I continued giving more details. 'The work you will do is not like anything you have done before.'

'I wouldn't say that,' he responded. I interrupted him because I had in my mind an image which I needed to describe while it was still clear. 'Let us be precise about this,' I rejoined. 'This work you have done in the past is similar to what you are now going to do, but it is not the same; and you will work with a material which you have not used before.'

'Well, yes,' he conceded. He was still surprised about my opening statement, and tried to choose his words carefully, almost stammering. Then he spoke firmly, 'I may as well tell you what it is that I am going to do'.

'No,' I broke in quickly. 'I will tell you.' A new image had presented itself in my mind, and I needed no distractions at that moment. As I turned my back on him and walked a few yards away the answer came to me. Turning, I pointed my finger at him. 'The material is fibre-glass and the objects to be made are boats,' I said.

Dave looked startled - lost for words. Cis found the situation delightfully amusing. Afterwards, she remarked that at the moment I gave my on-the-spot analysis, you could have bowled Dave over with the touch of a blade of grass. He departed muttering that he had better come and see me the following morning, so that I could predict the colour of the shirt he intended to wear! It was an episode of fun, pleasure and enlightenment.

Since then I have given Dave further readings from time to time. I am particularly interested and intrigued by future events which I see indicated in his life, for I like the man and I am anxious to see the outcome of actions he has yet to take.

In addition to his versatility and talent in craftsmanship Dave has the gift of being a natural healer. His spiritual disposition and instinct have led him to take a practical interest in remedial massage. I have no doubt of his ability to qualify in this specialisation; but most of his time and energy is devoted to his present work as a craftsman, which he must continue so as to meet his financial commitments.

My fear is that he may already be running out of time in which to make the most of his calling as a healer through the medium of remedial massage. Yet if he fails to respond to this call, he may regret it for the rest of his life.

Assessing one's potential

It is essential when determining your personal priorities to be aware of your potential, and to approach the question in a positive frame of mind. The satisfying sense of achievement which comes from the intuitive knowledge that you are on the right course can have a positive effect in fostering talent, since all traces of destructive negativeness have been removed.

I would like to tell you how one of my clients discovered this capacity for herself. Not only was she transformed completely by this awareness, but the consequences of the change which she experienced were of considerable importance to her.

Sonia Marchant had been to see me once for a consultation. A year-and-a-half later she brought along one of her friends who needed help with a personal matter. While she waited, Sonia told my lady companion, Cis, over a cup of tea, 'I thank Mr Ritson that I am here now. When I came here over a year ago I was very worried about my health. In the reading he gave me, Mr Ritson said that in the next year I would encounter health problems and have to go to hospital for two major operations. Well, he was right. I had cancer.'

I remember that as I had analysed Sonia's hand on that earlier occasion, the main symptom which caught my attention was an obvious weakness in health soon due to manifest itself in recognisable form. Hence my reference to hospital treatment. I was disturbed too that the illness seemed to pose a risk, but I did not say that she had cancer. My main concern was to tell my client that she should see a doctor, and reassure her as much as possible, before going on with my analysis to explore other features of interest.

I felt it would be improper to treat Sonia's imminent illness sketchily, as the indications were that she would be seriously ill in the near future. I asked no questions, but realised that she was unaware of the real nature of her illness. I felt that it was important to build up her confidence for the stresses she would have to face, and I believed that it would increase her confidence to remember the future time after her recovery, which I was able to describe.

'I did have to go into hospital and have two major operations, including radium treatment,' she told Cis. 'I felt very ill and thought I was going to die. When my family came to see me lying in my hospital bed, they tried to be cheerful. I could tell by their expressions that they did not think I would pull through, although no-one said this. After they left, and I was once more on my own, I gave into pain and simply lay there. Trying to think of something to take my mind off my suffering, I went back over all the things that had happened in my life since childhood, right up to the time I came to have my hand read by Mr Ritson.

'I suddenly thought to myself, 'What am I doing lying here thinking that I am going to die? The palmist told me that I would recover, and that my strength would return. He also told me what I would be doing with my life in five to six years' time.' From that moment onward I resolved to fight back and beat the disease which had a hold on me. Each time during my gradual recovery when I felt really ill I would think of his voice and what he had said to me. I am sure that if I had not had that reassurance to think about, I would have lain back in my bed, given up, and died. It gave me the will to fight back and to live.'

How brave of her! How correct her reasoning. Looking back now over what happened to Sonia, I see that it was right for her to come to see me in the first place, and it was the right time for her to do so. She was also infallibly correct in her decision to use her mind power to achieve a cure for her illness.

Today Sonia's life has a new purpose. As far as I know she is completely cured. She enjoys a full life in the company of her family. Her creative, independent spirit gives her the confidence to make the most she can of her life. She has a good job, many friends and a full social life, in conformity with her motto, 'life is for living'.

CHAPTER 16
Wisdom and Experience

I HAVE previously remarked on the cautious attitude of some clients, who are not necessarily sceptics, arising from the traditional fear associated with palmistry, and the power of the unknown. Despite the greater enlightenment of modern times, there are many clients who, before a consultation begins, ask me to tell them about their past only.

I answer, politely yet firmly, that they should not be unreasonable, that they already know enough of their past, and that they do not want to pay me merely to talk about past events. Yet the past can be very important, if it has a bearing on the future, or if it helps towards a greater understanding of themselves. My next step is to try to help them overcome the fear of what they might hear in an analysis, and to calm their apprehensions regarding knowledge of the future.

As we progress through life in an often hostile world, it is only to be expected that we should sometimes create hardships for ourselves, and afterwards wonder why we do this. The explanation is that for some reason either known or unknown to us, we are meant to go through such an experience or transition for our own good. Wisdom is not freely given. For most of us, it is earned by practical worldly experience; but some some people are endowed with a natural capacity to ask and speak wisely, arising no doubt from spiritual qualities which these individuals possess.

A person's life is not unlike a book, with phases divided into chapters. Each stage that we live through is a chapter in itself. Reflecting upon the events of their lives, some people may be unhappy with some of the chapters they have lived through. But closer investigation may bring a reminder that some of the most influential events of their lives occurred in periods covered by these very chapters. In other words they would not be where they are now in life, were it not for the events which they are unhappy to recall, but which formed a link with events in the next chapter. Chance does not arise. An event is simply meant to be, or it is not meant to be. I do not believe that there is any such thing as coincidence.

Let us examine the situation objectively. For example, were it not for the intervention of certain factors, a person would not have been in a certain place at a certain time which was essential as a link to a future sequence of events of extreme significance in their lives. The motivation behind such events is provided by the subtle and subjective working of destiny, which operates regardless of whatever plans the individual has made for his life. When the subjective and objective purposes are in harmony (when personal plans and destiny coincide) then the person concerned has found his or her true path in life.

We all have to pass various tests in life. It is not so much solving the problem that is important, but *how* we deal with the problem. Understanding this distinction can help someone who has been through a difficult period in life, and who may still have a difficult period to traverse, if the fates decree it.

In retrospect it is often possible to see that the obstacles we encountered were put there for a purpose. If it can be known in advance that a person will meet an obstacle at a certain point in the future, then steps can be taken to avoid it or at least decrease its damaging impact. When a client seeking a reading says to me, 'Please do not tell me anything bad,' it is clear that I cannot fully accede to this request. The ups-and-downs of the human condition are a necessary characteristic of life itself.

Karma, the Buddhist concept of the quality of actions (including the future impact of both those which are meritorious and less worthy, in predetermining the condition of all sentient beings), is allied to the experience which a person undergoes in the course of life. But individuals are responsible for their own actions, and karma cannot be entirely held to account for what happens to them. The state of wisdom attained by a person emerging from a period of acute suffering, or one who has come through a painful transition in life, can be seen as the central purpose in a person's striving to overcome obstacles and difficulties.

Apart from the role of karma, and the freedom to be responsible for oneself, spiritual law also has a part to play in deciding whether a person has earned merit or demerit by their actions. The human pathway through life seldom remains smooth for long; if it did so it would appear unnatural and shallow, and its limitations could lead to stagnation. An ideal civilisation could function for some time; but in time, evolution would bring about changes which would gradually alter conditions, through the operation of cosmic laws in the universe.

The development through the ages of the world, the whole universe (the macrocosm), follows a cosmic principle similar to that involved in the development of man, where both are ruled by Absolute or the God-head. If man is to be regarded as a model for, or epitome of, the universe (the microcosm) there is a spiritually functional affinity between himself, his creations and the universe as a whole; because outside the scale of both microcosm and macrocosm, one works within the other.

Common suffering

The common factor of suffering, whatever its cause, is its importance to those involved at the time. The end result in each episode of suffering must be understood and accepted, so that life can be resumed as normally as possible afterwards. The wisdom gained through each experience must be applied to fortify the individual against future repetitions of suffering. And if the many who have been through a similar experience unite and share their feelings, it should be possible to make the world a better place.

For another client, Elizabeth Hearn, the disruptive events threatening the peace of her world were just as important to her, personally, as weighty affairs of state might be to a government minister.

Elizabeth was accompanied by her sister, Joyce, who did not wish to have a consultation, and stayed with Cis in another room during the hand-reading. This was Elizabeth's first consultation with a palmist, and she did not know what to expect. The main problem, as seen from the line markings on her hand, was of a romantic nature. It could also be seen that Elizabeth was inclined to let her heart rule her head. The trial marriage in which she was then involved was an affair incorporating extremes of passion, lust and indifference, a whirlpool of conflicting emotions centering on the man in her life at that time.

Evidence of stress was clearly visible on Elizabeth's palm in the region of both the head line and heart line. Making allowances for her own fluctuations of mood, and by close inspection of the hand through my magnifying glass, I became convinced that it was not Elizabeth who was chiefly responsible for the stress patterns which I saw. It was more likely, I concluded, that she was the victim in a pattern of emotional disturbance initiated by her lover.

From the moment when my analysis began to explore the romantic areas of her life, my senses told me that Elizabeth was being subject to either mental cruelty, violence, or both through her lover's erratic behaviour. I told her about the signs I had noted. I described the personality of her lover, as I saw it, which it is possible to do in cases where one person has a strong affinity with another. This phenomenon often allows information regarding someone other than the person whose hand is being analysed to come to light. It adds an extra dimension to the client's capacity to communicate. Not only can her behaviour be seen through the signs on the hand, but changes resulting from the influences of others can also be identified. Where affinities exist between the client and others, these can either be harmonious and creative, or discordant and destructive.

When a person is being told something they do not wish to know, we can expect them to put up resistance. If my analysis shows that the client is resisting in this way, then I realise that the problem will be difficult to deal with because the person who needs help feels unable to co-operate. Often in situations of this kind, considerable time is spent in getting the client to see the need for an open-minded attitude, if the maximum advantage is to be gained from a consultation.

Destructive elements

Such was my task in the case of Elizabeth Hearn. Her situation was not improved by the nature of the man with whom she was involved. So in addition to difficulties resulting from her own attitude, there was the problem of her lover's influence over her.

While their relationship could be interpreted palmistically as a trial marriage, my reading showed strong destructive elements, which confirmed that the liaison would not last. Seeing this crisis point approaching in her immediate future, I urged her repeatedly to think seriously about not entering into a further reconciliation with such an unsuitable partner.

Elizabeth then spoke for the first time during the reading. She was in agreement with my overall analysis. I saw a change of home which would be good for her, and emphasised the point that she should now take complete control over her finances and in future keep everything that was legally hers in her own name.

Though she agreed with what I said, I was not altogether convinced of the strength of her intentions. Promises were one thing, deeds another. I feared that against her own good judgement, she would yield to her weaker feelings and give her lover yet another opportunity to betray her. Now was the time for her to sever the relationship.

When the reading was over, we rejoined her sister, Joyce, and my lady companion, Cis. On seeing her, Cis remarked that Elizabeth's appearance had changed in contrast to the way she had looked before entering the consulting-room. Elizabeth turned to me and said, 'Your reading has been surprisingly accurate, Mr Ritson. You were so right about what you saw for me, and to prove it, I would like to show you some photographs.' What I saw there shocked me, and it took a few moments for me to understand what I was seeing. I held in my hand a series of coloured photographs of a woman who had been a victim of a savage, barbaric beating. Her physical state was such that she was almost unrecognisable. It was Elizabeth, some months before the reading.

Her damaged features were distorted by a hideous mass of bruises, abrasions and mutilations, including two black eyes, a broken nose and further damage suggesting a fractured jaw. The skin of her back from her shoulders to her waist was raw and excoriated. 'If the police had not broken into the house, he would have killed her,' Elizabeth's sister commented. The photographs were taken by the police as evidence of the crime.

This terrible attack took place on an evening when Elizabeth had gone with her lover to a local dance. It seems that on arriving there it was usual for the man to settle Elizabeth down alone in a corner of the dance hall, while he went off and danced with other women. It was not acceptable to him that Elizabeth also should have the right to dance with other partners. Whenever she did so, he over-reacted by a display of extreme wrath and jealousy.

On this occasion, when she had sat on her own for a considerable time, Elizabeth told the man that she was going home. As the house she owned was within reasonable walking distance she collected her coat and left the dance hall.

When she arrived home and opened the front door she found that her lover was already in the house, waiting for her. He immediately seized her and proceeded mercilessly to beat her up, having made sure that the front door was securely locked by its trip-catch mechanism. Neighbours who heard her cries and screams called the police and she was taken to hospital.

Because I was interested in discovering what kind of man could treat a woman in this way, I asked Elizabeth if she had a sample of his handwriting available, such as a letter. It so happened that she had a letter which he had written, in her handbag. I explained that I had some knowledge and practical experience of graphology, which is the art of assessing personality and character from a study of a person's handwriting. The style of writing peculiar to this man confirmed my view of him as an individual of disturbed mind and unstable temperament. My description of the man drew the comment from Joyce that I seemed to know him as well as if I had met him.

As a layman in medical matters, I suspected that Elizabeth's lover might be suffering from schizophrenia, a serious functional disorder increasingly believed to be due to organic brain damage. I felt that he needed psychiatric help, and that the nature of his crime, together with the photographic evidence of its horrific effect, must surely call for medical assessment; but I do not know what action was taken in this regard.

When Elizabeth came out of hospital she went to stay with her sister. Joyce was naturally very concerned about Elizabeth's future and in front of Cis and me, told her 'No way can you go back to him. He nearly killed you this time, and if there were a next time, it is too great a risk to consider.'

For a moment Elizabeth rallied to her man's defence. 'Whenever he maltreats me, he gets down on his knees afterwards, crying and pleading for my forgiveness. And at other times he really can be so nice.' But despite these sentiments, by the time she left us later that afternoon, Elizabeth knew in her heart what she must do. The plan was that for the time being she would stay with her sister, Joyce. Because of her ordeal, Elizabeth was no longer happy about living in her own home and had, I believe, made arrangements to sell the property.

For her part, Joyce was pleased that she had brought Elizabeth to me for a consultation. Before leaving she said that both the hand-reading and the graphology had proved a point to her sister that the only rational decision for her was not to be reunited with her former lover. I was sure also that Joyce would stand by Elizabeth to whatever extent was necessary to help her shape a new life for herself.

Touching lightly again on the subject of schizophrenia, I should point out that it is not correct to describe this condition in terms of a 'split mind'. We all have 'split mind' tendencies, in so far as what we say and what we do are quite often at odds with each other.

Handwriting analysis

My interest in handwriting analysis arises because writing is, so to speak, an extension of the hand itself. I do not refer to graphology very often when giving consultations to clients who see me exclusively as a palmist clairvoyant. Palmistry and clairvoyance are my first love. But graphology can be valuable in confirming impressions about a person's nature, ability, will-power and sexual strength, which have already been revealed through hand-reading, intuition or extra-sensory perception.

There was an instance when one of my clients brought me hand-prints of their daughter, together with a specimen of her handwriting for analysis. The results obtained were accurate and useful to the young lady, whom I shall call Julia.

I discovered that she had a choice of two potentially successful careers open to her. Her first choice was a career which would appeal only temporarily. In time she would wish to turn to work of more lasting significance which was better suited to her temperament. Indeed, signs of the impending transition were already evident in Julia's approach to life. I learned later that she had begun to study medicine, but was then drawn towards work which gave opportunities for travel and language study.

Both in Julia's hand-prints and in her handwriting I could

discern some tension arising from pressures in her romantic life. It appeared to me that she was concerned to ensure that a valued relationship with her boy-friend should survive, and I also pointed out very clearly that the situation did not rest with herself alone. Her boy-friend would also have something to say, though he would not give her what is termed the 'brush off'.

I subsequently learned that some time after my analysis, Julia's boy-friend suggested that she should go abroad to pursue her interest in foreign languages, and that she should enjoy her freedom for a while. He told her that he would maintain contact with her during her absence and while he completed his university studies. On graduation, he would ask her how she now felt about their relationship and the idea of a life together.

I could see a successful career stretching into the future for Julia, provided that she kept up a high standard in her work and followed up her interest in linguistics. Palmistically she showed the ability to succeed well. Another interesting sign was that her future expertise in linguistics would place her in line for work as a political specialist or in a supportive role in politics.

Time will tell how accurate my predictions have been. If her future life could be said to resemble a book, then it is one with a great many blank pages. And it is up to Julia to apply her undoubted intelligence and sensitivity in writing the next chapters. At another time and in another place, she would encounter the correct atmosphere for retrospect, but the calling now acting within her regarding her career prospects was too strong for her sensibly to deny.

CHAPTER 17
Early Predictions

LOOKING back and recalling to mind past events in our lives is a common practice. Usually, we have little difficulty in recapturing moments of special significance which have a special place in one's memory. Recollections of an early love, of a particularly memorable day, of an exciting event - these are the stuff of which nostalgia is made.

If you talk to a person aged seventy years or more, it is more than likely that the conversation will turn at some stage to things past, and life as it used to be in his or her own young days.

It is understandable that we should relate the style and conditions of our own lives to those of our fathers and grandfathers, even great-grandfathers, because of the habit of association. Clearly it is easier for the average person to look back in time than to analyse creatively their prospects in the years ahead, and to look forward to the era of the generation to come. The past has its importance, not least that it contains within its roots the factors out of which effective change has been created. But to live in the past too much is to assume a too negative approach to life, and to its values.

There will always be critics who from their own standpoint can argue logically against any tide of change, always confident that things should have remained as they were; but this reasoning is blind and militates against the laws of nature. It could be said that the quality of life was better for certain people in the days before the industrial revolution and the internal combustion engine, in the period before 1914 and large-scale mechanisation, and in the days before the destruction wrought by two world wars.

The early twentieth century marked a period of transition from a situation where man had to make a living by the sweat of his brow to one where the choices on offer included working towards a higher purpose, and a personal awareness in mental, physical and spiritual terms. Since each new period of evolution is more advanced than the preceding one, it may be unwise to linger too long over the past, and wiser to live for now and the future.

Children's hands

About thirteen years ago, for my own interest, I made a private study of the hands of some young children up to seven years of age. I found that the majority of youngsters possessed the capacity to be analytical, calculating and readily adaptable to meet the practical and scientific demands of life. In a contest for the survival of the strongest among them, a self- motivating driving force was clearly evident. In the hyper-active this tended to lead to behaviour problems, such as uncontrollability and restlessness and health risks of a possibly nervous type.

I also saw in the children's hands an indifference or unawareness when it came to situations meriting self-discipline, or where they needed to be confronted with discipline. Their self-confidence, I felt, derived more from their own use of their freedom. But the formations of most of the heart lines I examined showed a tendency to stubbornness and some aggression when a situation called for expression of emotion. Overall, it seemed from my study that the young had a purpose to express a new search for personal identity compatible with the new age into which they were born, and relevant to the age ahead of them.

Computer technology is now part of today's educational curriculum and is willingly accepted by the young developing mind. The pattern of home-life for the young has changed radically. It is now usual for youngsters to have a room of their own equipped in every way to make them detached from other members of the family if they so wish. Their bedroom becomes their bed-sit; such is the modern trend. The hands of teenagers are not easy to interpret; they can be both provoking and challenging. Whereas it is possible to inform them of their potential through a hand-reading, they may not take the path best suited to them because of their temperament or their restless search for novelty and variety.

When Anthony Lucas first came to me he was on the threshold of a career which could have led to success as a banker or an economist. I could see from his hand markings that he was of high intelligence and that a feature of his character at the time was a suppressed intensity of feeling which registered in his subconscious. While this intensity was, I felt, a forceful factor, it needed to be released and expressed; if restrained it would lead to a troubled emotional life.

Examining Anthony's career potential in relation to banking and industrial economy, I saw what appeared to be a break of two years in the continuity of his working life. This suggested a temporary distraction taking him away from his declared purpose, and leading in an altogether different direction. I told him what I saw in his hand.

Anthony then said that having obtained a good number of GCE 'O' and 'A' level passes, he had gone to university. With his studies now completed, he intended to hitch-hike round the world for the next two years. He was particularly interested in going to India, to find out about the country's culture and its impact on him personally.

I asked him if he would like to know in advance what the outcome of the experience would be. He said that he would, so I told him that the two-year period he planned to spend wandering would be of little benefit to him. The idea of foreign travel was premature and impractical at the time. I emphasised the importance of his concentrating on basic needs. He should develop his career first, and become firmly established in it. Later, there would be time for him to respond to the urge to wander further afield. And it would no longer be a case of following haphazard leads here and there. He would be able to set out with a firm sense of purpose, and a better knowledge of the countries he visited.

I did not see Anthony again until two years later. The intensity which I had previously observed was still evident, and his mood showed signs of exasperation. Despite my advice, he had in the interval persisted with his ambition to travel round the world. He had visited India, but had failed to find the inspiration he sought in Eastern philosophy or an Eastern way of life. Consequently he was disenchanted.

Examining his palm once more, I told him that his immediate future featured a re-entry into the pattern of living which he understood best. He smiled when he heard this, and explained that he had accepted an offer which to all intents and purposes meant a resumption of his original career in banking and economics.

Anthony's attempt to shape a destiny for himself other than the one intended for him explained the break in continuity which I had seen in his hand. The life-style which he finally adopted was, as far as I could tell, the right choice for him. He was now in effect two years behind schedule, and it remained to be seen if he could make up for the time spent fruitlessly on a search for which he was not ready at that point in his life.

I have a simple purpose in my approach to every reading. It is the desire for accuracy. When an accurate reading can be established beyond doubt, it proves that the system of palmistry or clairvoyance works effectively. While I do not set out to convert a client to a different viewpoint as a result of my reading, I do aim to provide convincing evidence through palmistic and extra- sensory means. This approach can confirm the existence of an established pattern of thoughts and actions in a client's make-up; or it may provide guidelines for laying down new patterns. It is rewarding in its own way when my predictions are proved correct with the client's co-operation.

It could be said that I am well-known in my district. Clients come to me from all over Europe and as far afield as Africa. Yet it is sometimes when working with clients from areas nearer home that I have the satisfaction of seeing a happy prophecy come true.

One evening, as I waited for our trolley of groceries to be checked out at a large supermarket, I noticed a couple who joined the adjacent queue. I recognised the women opposite me as a client whom I had not seen for a consultation for some time. Inevitably our eyes met, and for a short while we exchanged glances. Initially, I refrained from acknowledging the woman openly, because I was not sure if she wished it to be known that I knew her in my capacity as a palmist clairvoyant.

I am aware that some clients are secretive about their visits to me for consultation, probably because they wish to avoid criticism from others who dismiss palmistry and mediumship as forms of hocus-pocus. As the woman continued to look in my direction I greeted her politely and she left her companion to come and speak to me. She was Felicity Shepherd, whom I had known as a client for a few years. When we last met she was divorced and her zest for living had been nearly extinguished by post-divorce depression. At that time she was lonely, and although protective towards her children, had reached a stage where she needed to have a man in her life. Yet she lacked the self-confidence to avail herself of an opportunity for romance, were it to come her way.

My hand-reading revealed that destiny had a second marriage in store for Felicity in the near future. Her response to this information was hesitant. She was not in the right frame of mind to be prepared to believe in my prediction, or in her own capacity to make a new relationship. Privately, I hoped that she did not let the chance slip away when it was offered, because to be involved in another romantic failure could undermine her self-confidence, once and for all. After the consultation she left, prepared to give me the benefit of the doubt but still low in spirit.

In the interval between that last consulation and this chance meeting, time had wrought beneficial changes in Felicity's personal appearance, and in her mental and emotional outlook. Her eyes sparkled audaciously, and she had regained her warmth of personality. I wondered if she was still a member of a certain operatic and drama group for, if so, her success in this field seemed assured.

The good news she gave me was that she was married again. There was no need to ask if she was happy. Her companion, who turned out to be her new husband, had been watching suspiciously while we talked. The expression in his eyes when he looked at me showed what I thought was protective jealousy. I felt sure that he did not know who I was, and that he was probably wondering what attraction there was between us.

I congratulated Felicity and asked her if the man in the queue was her husband. 'Yes, yes,' she replied, 'and he's ever so lovely.'

'How nice for you,' I said, watching him watching me. He was nearly six feet tall and casually dressed. Before she rejoined him, I wished her a happy future with her man. She recalled the last hand-reading I had given her and said how pleased she was that my forecast had proved correct, and that she and her husband had found each other.

'Tell him,' I said, 'that he came into your life merely as a little mark upon your hand.'

Certain clients whom Cis and I have known for many years have become close friends. One such friend is Winifred Townsend, who came to me for a reading thirteen years ago. Both her hands had long and expressive head-lines, showing that she possessed a strong analytical mind, and considerable mental energy. Her directness could be off-putting to those who did not understand her disposition. By nature she was an eternal giver. But she could be self-conscious and guarded when it was her turn to receive recognition, appreciation or love from others.

As I examined her palms at that first analysis I realised that Winifred was exceptionally psychic and intuitive, although she made no reference to these qualities as she waited for my assessment. The sensation I experienced then can be simply explained. I was conscious of being in the presence of a person much superior to myself and more worthy of respect. Looking back to that meeting, I can see that it served as a testing point for me in terms of my awareness and career development. Upon her hands I could see clearly the line of intuition and a mark known in palmistry as *la croix mystique.*

At the time I did not know enough to be able to discuss the matter fully and I said so. 'You are more advanced than myself,' I told Winifred. 'I cannot tell you anything that you do not already know. In fact, because of your greater knowledge, you could give me information and advice. I had not used the words 'psychic' or 'intuition' in speaking to her. We were both immediately aware of the qualities we had in common and although I was not fully conscious of its complications at the time, the fact that I had acknowledged her powers and symbolically saluted her, was sufficient as a beginning.

An important clue to Winifred's powers lay in the relationship between the length of her head-line and the placing of *la croix mystique* adjacent to it. The main factor confirming the range and power of her spiritual gifts and shrewd insight was the presence on her right hand of the Ring of Solomon seen around one of the mounts of the palm - the Mount of Saturn.

The implication of this cluster of symbols was that this was a woman whose energy, power and wisdom were drawn to mysticism and occultism. In the pursuit of knowledge this dedication placed superstition in a lesser category, and directed the moving force of mental energy towards the mastery of even higher levels of knowledge and attainment.

Winifred appreciated my openness. Our friendship was already developing. During that evening she disclosed to Cis and me that she knew beforehand that she would meet us in the way she did, in order that a special link could be forged between the three of us. Then she told us that there existed in our home the spirit of a girl who had appeared to her during the reading with me. This not uncommon phenomenon had interesting consequences for Cis and me.

The story of Poll Miles

A few months later we heard for the first time a local legend about a young girl who had lived in our village during the early or mid-eighteenth century. Her name was Poll Miles, and her home was none other than the cottage we occupied.

The story of Poll Miles is factual in that she was a real person and not just the product of romantic imaginations. Her life was short as she died at seventeen.

Poll was born in our cottage but her parents separated while she was very young, and she lived with her father from the age of eight years onwards. She chose to live close to nature and, following her mother's teaching, she continued to learn about herbs and their uses as cures and remedies.

Then she fell in love with Joe Scott, a groom who served the gentry at the nearby castle, which is a noted landmark. It is said that Poll and Joe pledged eternal love for one another. But local superstition insisted that Poll was the daughter of a witch and was doubtless one herself also. When rumours of this kind reached Joe Scott, he allowed gossip, prejudice and fear to influence his feelings towards Poll. He transferred his affections to a French maid who served at the castle.

At a Christmas Eve dance with all the villagers present, Poll beheld Joe in the arms of her rival. Deeply hurt and distraught at the loss and his betrayal, she was heard to utter threats against them. She then left the dance and was never seen alive again.

Eleven weeks later Poll's body was found floating in a canal, still in the red dress she had worn at the dance. No final verdict was reached as to whether her death was due to suicide or foul play. After some debate she was eventually buried at the parish boundary beneath a mound set to one side of a crossroads. Tradition has it that for many years flowers were regularly placed on her grave at each Hallowe'en.

Today, Poll Miles is commemorated on the colourful village sign which stands on a green site. A ballad about her was included recently in a long-playing record by a local folk group. Her legend lives on.

Winifred Townsend, who first brought Poll's story to our attention, is still a most valued friend. Through the years she has been a great help to me, aiding me considerably by her knowledge and wisdom, which I recognised at our first meeting. Her parents were friends of Sir Arthur Conan Doyle; and Winifred - now in her seventies - remembers meeting him when she was a little girl.

Many of these first clients whom I saw in my early years still visit me for consultations. This fact, in itself, says much to me. By returning again and again, these clients pay me a compliment. But there are difficulties to be expected if care is not taken when working with friends.

My personal discipline demands that I maintain a detached view on every occasion that I give them a hand analysis. I have to put out of my mind everything I already know about them. I also have to ignore the effects of previous predictions for my client, in making an objective analysis. In other words, I have to look at the familiar person as if I were seeing him or her for the first time.

Mine own consultant

I am frequently asked whether or not I can read my own palm. The answer is that I can, but I do not often take it upon myself to be mine own consultant. When I choose to do so, I find it a useful exercise to palmistically trace from various line markings what my future holds for me.

In order to obtain deeper analysis, I get into a frame of mind where I examine my hand as though it were not my own, which calls for a certain discipline.

Clairvoyance is a gift. It is a most ancient craft, and those who hold this power understand they cannot use this extra-sensory perception for guidance in the shaping of their own destiny. All the clairvoyants I have known, some of exceptional calibre, are unable to use their psychic ability with regard to themselves, which is no less than the fundamental working of a spiritual law.

In a different category there is the power of positive thought, used by many. Their success depends upon whether they have sufficient electromagnetism to assist them. A person with the appropriate amount of positive energy and having the correct mental approach can train and strengthen their positive mind, so that in due course what they set out to achieve can in all probability come to pass.

In practical terms, positive thought can apply as simply as when a person realises that he or she has the correct degree of sensitivity in perceiving, say, an ambition or purpose. In a person's own words this heightened sense of awareness might be expressed as 'I had a feeling that particular thing would work.'

Everyone can experience intuition, which functions like a 'still voice' in the mind, but is not in the same realm as clairvoyance. I am personally acquainted with the sensation of *déjà vu*, a French term meaning 'already seen', or in other words the feeling that one has been there before. When this happens, I experience the dual sensation of seeing something for the first time, and simultaneously being aware that the situation is very familiar. It is as if I were reliving the moment as it takes place. These occasions are when 'chronos' (time in chronological order) becomes 'cairos' (the eternal now).

Future is born out of the crest of the now. If a person can survive the next five seconds in time, then from that point, for him, creative future begins. The quintessence of creative future is vitality, important as life itself. The lines upon the human hand record the various degrees of vitality, possessed in different levels by different individuals. Vitality is channelled in turn towards certain effects, thus contributing to a person's proficiency in one direction or another.

Revelations produced through palmistry and clairvoyance can be used to illuminate the creative potential of a person's vitality. It is through this vitality that the individual is able to gain a better understanding of the aims set for him, and of the means of achieving them.

I would assert that enlightenment and learning are either correctly used or at their best only when a balance is maintained between instinct and intelligence. The development of man's consciousness began with the use of his instinct alone, from which his intelligence evolved. Wonderful and fascinating though our modern world may be, due to the many technological advances which we have created and enjoy, we should nevertheless avoid becoming too enamoured with intellect. We must not risk ignoring the mental aspect of those actions which rank between unconscious reflex activities and intelligent conduct. A quality of life determined by intelligence alone would lack spiritual completeness; but paired with instinct, the effect would be to broaden our horizon, and offer a richer manner of living to those willing to avail themselves of it.

I find an increasing number of business people among my clients. What they all tend to have in common is the need to know if the path they are pursuing in commerce is the best one, not only to safeguard existing assets, but to lead most rapidly to financial success.

One such client is Edward Jansen. I established that his particular talent was in salesmanship; and to date, I have been correct in all my forecasts concerning him. His shrewd mode of thought, combined with dynamic driving power, continue to serve him well. When he as the seeker and I as the seer meet in consultation, we immdiately achieve a distinct harmony. Through my guidance over the years, in matters concerned with decision making and the exploration of new creative outlets, he has become both a ready and appreciative participant in the art of divinatory palmistry. Recently, I predicted that he would set up his own business, connected with the sale and distribution of non-perishable foods.

A man of an altogether different type is Geoffrey Hardcastle. My psychical exploration of his world of strange contrasts uncovered the enigma of an individual talented and creative on the one side, but profound and melancholic on the other.

The personality and character of Hardcastle, and the force of his individuality, would probably gain approval among those whose concept of life and its purposes has no place for the man content with a simple life-style. Contentment, in their eyes, can be the first stage in stagnation, and therefore must be challenged. Life is constantly changing and contentment, in their view, is transient. It was in Hardcastle's nature to challenge everything he came into contact with, oscillating between the desire to be part of society, and at the same time to shun it, retreating into a world of his own. I suspect he would be more at home with animals than people.

An expert in the world of antiques and paintings, Hardcastle's knowledge has earned widespread admiration. Yet he is plagued by self-doubt, and can be completely irrational in his behaviour. Moreover, having a penchant for alcohol, he often knowingly drinks too heavily. Unfortunately he has shown a marked inability to hold permanently to a romantic relationship, although this difficulty may have been partly due to the type of women with whom he had affairs.

He is well aware of the rewards and improved status which could be his quite easily, and I have warned him about the dangers of his lapsing into a chaotic state of personal hostility, physical and moral ruin. But sadly, he seems determined to follow the downward self-destructive path rather than save himself.

Another client in difficulties is Andrew Fitzgerald, a young and talented musician. Having the stamp of the perfectionist, he is at present undergoing a period of frustration in his quest for a place at the top in his profession. Having re-formed his group of musicians and taken it upon himself to perform also as lead singer, he is heading straight into the precarious world of popular music. But he has the stamina and vision for such an undertaking. Given the necessary good fortune, he should, I predict, soon emerge as a successful composer, lyricist and front-line musician.

It remains to be seen with the passing of time how the respective life-styles of these three - the businessman, the antiques expert, and the aspiring musician - will evolve. And time will also tell how well they each accept their lot.

Acceptance, in terms of agreement to whatever life offers, is an option open to all of us, whether we be fatalists or fighters. We are all creatures of change, answering that which surrounds us, or responding to an instinct which is not always irrational, embodied perhaps in something that is original and free in expression.

The summit is for us the personal achievement of the same form as the power which creates and regulates the material world, the power of growth, and that our own aspirations should conform with it, by the grace of God, the Absolute. Within the hand of man and within the powers of his mind are the keys to the universe.

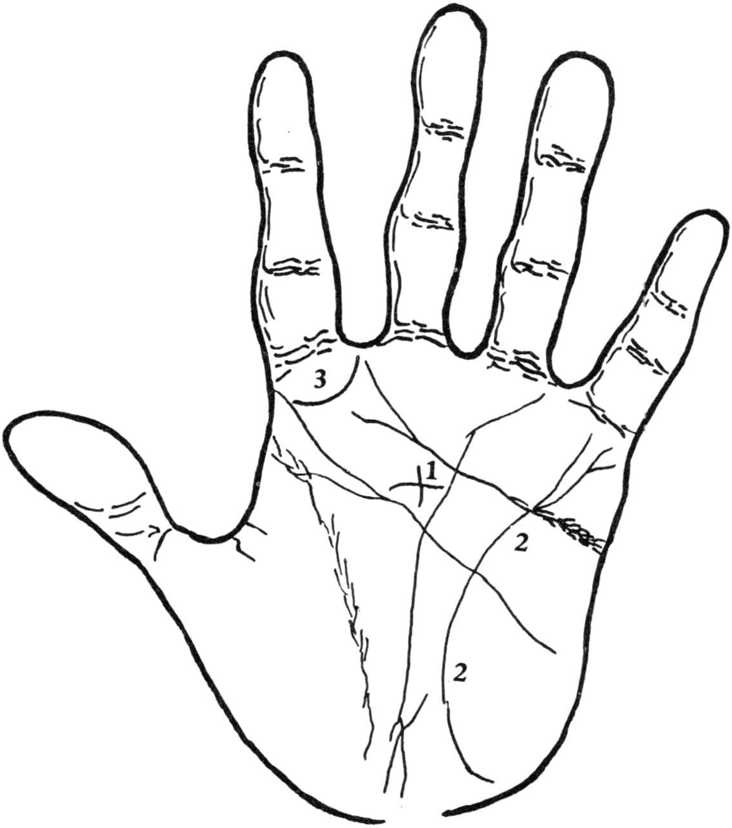

An example of a hand showing:
1 *La croix mystique*
2 The Line of Intuition
3 The Ring of Solomon

La croix mystique signifies superstition, mysticism, and involvement with the occult, and with the secret world, transcending the bounds of natural knowledge. When positioned upon the hand closer to the Line of Heart than the Line of Head, this indicates a superstitious nature, and even more so if positioned over the centre of the Line of Head. The longer the Line of Head accompanied by *la croix mystique*, the greater is the indication that the person will be drawn increasingly into occultism throughout life.

The Line of Intuition is represented upon the hand in the form of a semi-circular curve which traverses the region extending from the Mount of Mercury to the Mount of Moon or Luna. Persons whose hands bear this mark are highly sensitive to everything going on around them. They are very impressionable. They have strong intuitive feelings where others are concerned, which act in contrast with a call to meditation. Their dreams tend to become reality. They do not believe in coincidence.

The Line of Intuition signifies an alliance with a state of mental awareness bordering on the psychic. Palmistically, it shows close alliance to the mark, *la croix mystique.*

The Ring of Solomon denotes admiration for the power of the occult, and a strong capacity to learn more of its secrets. So marked is this tendency that the person with this mark can acquire the power of the master, and become adept in this particular science. The Ring of Solomon could be described as a superior mark to *la croix mystique.*

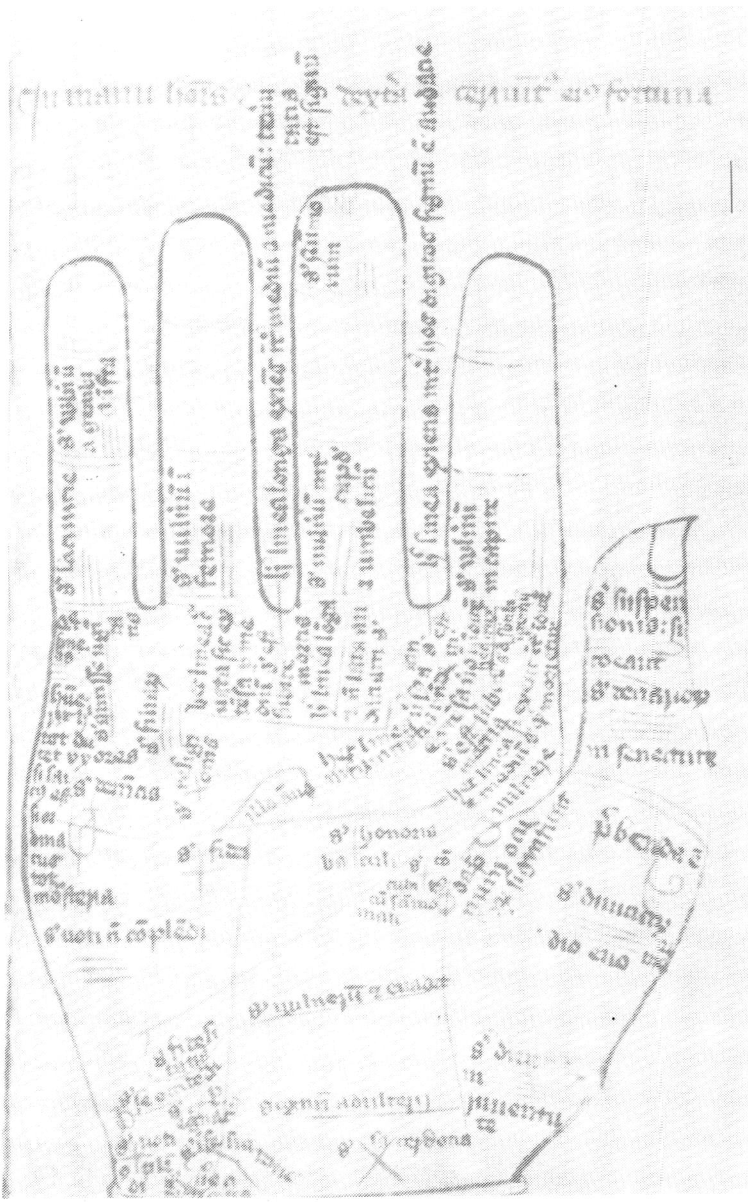

A late 14th century drawing of a hand, from the Summa Chiromantia.

CHAPTER 18
A Short History of Palmistry

PALMISTRY is of considerable antiquity and the country held to be its birthplace is India. Hindus of the Joshi caste, known for their knowledge of the occult, produced chirological writings amongst their sacred records and holy books two thousand years or more before Christ. The wisdom of the Hindus spread to other parts of the world and chirology was extensively practised in other countries such as China, Tibet, Persia, Mesopotamia and Greece, where it found especial favour.

Palmistry in its present form derives from Greece, where it was given the title of Cheiromancy, from the Greek word *heri*, meaning the hand. The oldest known treaty on palmistry entitled *De Historia Animalium* was written by Aristotle (384–322 BC), the most famous of the Greek philosophers, and a disciple of Plato. Pliny refers to palmistry in his *Natural History*, and Anaxagoras both practised and taught the science of palmistry.

A legend reputed to be authentic, says of Aristotle that when he undertook the education of Alexander (356-323 BC) - later known as Alexander the Great - he sent his pupil an Arabic treatise on the hand which he had discovered during his travels in Egypt. The book, written in letters of gold, was found upon an altar dedicated to Hermes. The treatise was sent to young Alexander as a study worthy of an elevated and enquiring mind, and was subsequently translated from the Arabic into Latin by Hispanus.

During the Renaissance palmistic skills were considered a legitimate part of natural science until they met with opposition from the Church. Cheirology was thus condemned and driven underground. The Romany, close to nature and respecting the science and the art of the hand, kept alive traditions and techniques associated with hand reading, which originated in Spain.

The oldest known palmistic document written in the English language and dated before 1440, is the *Digby Roll* IV in the Bodleian Library, Oxford. In Germany, as Gutenberg was developing a printing press, one of the first books ever printed

△ *The decorative frontispiece from Ludicrum Chirimanticum, published in Jena in 1661.*

◁ *A woodcut from Cocles' book on chiromancy, depicting a 16th century palmistry consultation.*

(despite persecution from the Church), was a work on palmistry by Johann Hartlieb, entitled *Die Kunst Ciromantia*, which was printed in Augsburg in 1475. This was the first of many books produced on the subject. Michael Scott's *De Phisiognomia* of 1477 included in its text details of chirognomy, the meanings derived from the shapes of the hand, fingers and skin texture.

Through the centuries additional works were produced by many intelligent and respected people. Towards the end of the nineteenth century palmistry was given additional impetus through the work of two Frenchmen, Casimir Stanislas D'Arpentigny, who concentrated on cheirognomic aspects of the science, and Adrien Adolphe Desbarrolles, who was an authority on cheiromancy.

An eminent anatomist, Sir Charles Bell, was the author of the famous *Bridgewater Treatise* on the hand, in which he said, 'We cannot feel the pulse with the tongue but we can with the fingers. The hand belongs exclusively to man, corresponding in sensibility and motion to the endowment of his mind.'

One of the most admired and remarkable figures in the history of cheiromancy, a man of renowned ability, was Count Louis Hamon, who practised under the name of Cheiro. The study of most aspects of the occult absorbed him until his death in 1936.

In more recent times, Julius Spier produced work on psycho-cheirology involving studies of the hands of both children and of mentally disordered people. This work inspired Dr. Carl Gustav Jung to engage in further study of cheirology, including it in the total conception of modern biology.

1 *A page from Die Kunst Ciromantia, by Johann Hartlieb, which was published in Augsburg in 1475, from the British Museum.*

2 *A page from Saunder's Palmistry - The Secrets Thereof Disclosed, his second book, published in 1664*

3 *The frontispiece to Johann Ingeber's Chiromantia, Metoposcopia et Physiognomia, published in 1698.*

4 *A simple woodcut from Cocles' Ciromantia.*

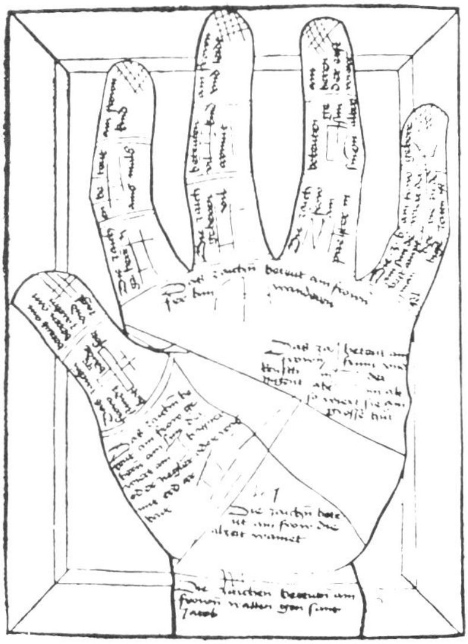

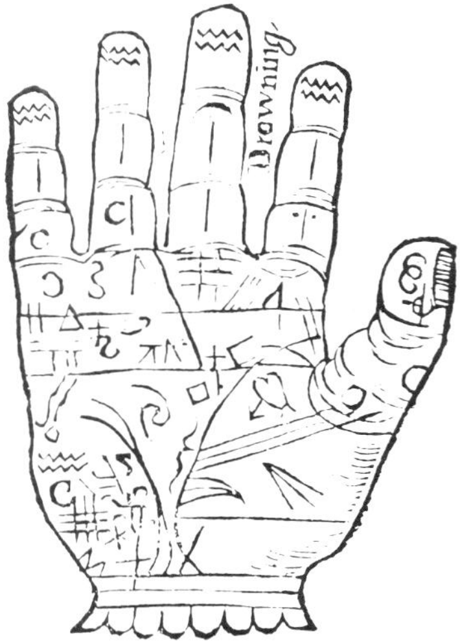

Drowning

1 2

3 4

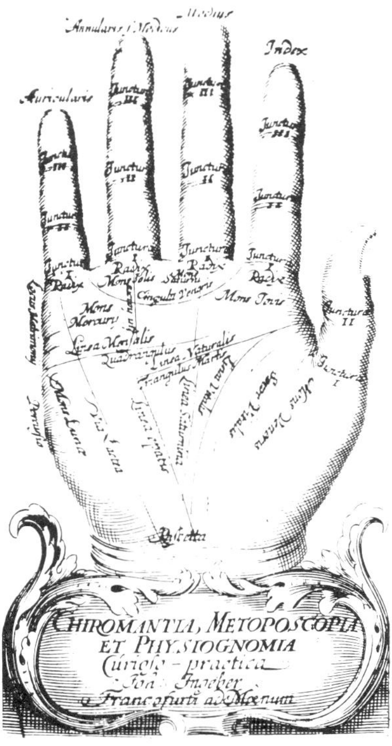

Medius
Annularis / Medius
Index
Auricularis
Mons Solis
Cingulum Veneris
Mons Jovis
Linea Mensalis
Linea Naturalis
CHIROMANTIA, METOPOSCOPIA
ET PHYSIOGNOMIA
Curioso - practica
Francofurti ad Moenum